THINK DESIGN LIVE

THINK DESIGN LIVE

Unblock Your Mind and Live Your Dreams

Pialee Mukherjee

Book cover design and graphics by Rutajeet Mukherjee
Book interior design by Prashant Kumar
Indexing by Neelam Gupta

ISBN- 978-93-5396-134-3
PURPLE INK Imprint

To
The Source
of
All that IS

Men are so entranced by
The tree
That they have forgotten
The seed,
The source of the tree.
Forgetting the source is what
Keeps men from
The Source.

Wu Hsin

Contents

Introduction 1

Chapter One
Mind Matters 5

Chapter Two
Living by Default 15

Chapter Three
You Can Design Your Life 25

Chapter Four
Change Begins With a Thought 35

Chapter Five
Define Your Success 45

Chapter Six
The Subconscious Can Block Your Success   59

Chapter Seven
Uncover Your Hidden Blocks   73

Chapter Eight
Rewire and Redesign   87

Chapter Nine
Dream to Reality: Living in Your Garden of Life   105

Chapter Ten
GPS Your Destination: Enjoy Your
Journey Ahead   119

Acknowledgments   135

Resources   137

Index   139

About Author   151

Reflections   153

Introduction

If you are always trying to be normal, you will never know how amazing you can be.

Maya Angelou

If this book has found its way to you, you are about to discover how amazing your life can be. As humans, we all look for meaning in life, searching constantly for an answer to the question, "Why am I here?" We want to know what the point of it all is, and how we can make our time here on earth relevant and meaningful. It is understood that knowledge is potential power but I would like to add that it is only when you have knowledge of 'Self' can you lead a truly empowered life.

This book attempts to help you understand yourself better—your motivations, your uniqueness, your needs and desires, your dream for yourself and the life you would love to live, and what is holding you back or blocking you from it. You will find transformational tools that enable you to design your own life, by breaking through your mental and emotional blocks and stuck states, enabling you to live a life of purpose and fulfillment. Deeper aspects are laid out in very simple ways with the use of examples, analogies and real life stories, as well as step-by-step guidelines.

How we handle our thoughts is directly proportional to how we live our life. Throughout the book you are encouraged to *think* and find your own answers. Instead of reading it passively you will derive the most value if you engage with it. At the end of the book there are worksheets where you can write down your reflections. *Think Design Live: Unblock Your Mind and Live Your Dreams* is designed to be your own personal friend and guide, holding up the mirror for you. It is developed from years of study, practice, training, mentoring, sharing and personal growth.

The initial chapters are designed to help you understand how the quality of our thought affects our lives at various levels; how they shape the reality we live; and how one can consciously direct them to shape a meaningful reality where we can thrive and be truly joyful. Further, you are encouraged to question your existing life and look at it honestly. Look at the gaps, because only when you acknowledge there is a chasm, between where you are and where you want to be, will you attempt to build the bridge. The final chapters take you through the action steps which will help you consciously create a purpose-filled life.

As you process the ideas presented in the book and experiment with them in your daily life, it will help you evolve from thinking, to doing, to being able to live a version of yourself that you always wanted. The person who reaches the end of this book will not be the same person who began reading it.

CHAPTER ONE

Mind Matters

Though I do not believe that a plant will spring up where no seed has been, I have great faith in a seed. …Convince me that you have a seed there, and I am prepared to expect wonders.

Henry David Thoreau

When we wake up to the mysteries of our mind, our reality begins to shift. I invite my readers to become childlike once more and open your mind to the wondrous possibilities that life has to offer and reawaken in you the curiosity and enthusiasm you once had. Let us go on this journey of learning, experimenting, growing, and becoming.

Keep Your Mind Open

Today learning is exponential. At the tip of our fingers, there is so much access to knowledge and information, it is phenomenal. Knowledge is like a seed that holds enormous potential. A seed might either grow into a beautiful flowering plant, a medicinal herb, a fully-laden fruit tree, or it might grow into a dreaded poisonous plant, a thorny bush or a creeper, amongst several other possibilities. But when buried underground the seed is not visible; it is not yet manifest. If you want to consciously create a garden for yourself, you will select seeds with care, and you will not randomly plant whatever seeds are available to you.

The potential of the seed is manifest with careful, consistent, patient, and informed nurturing. Preparing the soil, watering, tending, pruning, de-weeding, with care and patience, the seed of a rose plant blossoms to its fullest potential when it flowers into a beautiful, colourful, fragrant rose, or the seed of a *neem* tree manifests into a full-grown tree that gives shade, purifies the atmosphere or its leaves used for medicinal purposes.

If you keep a seed preserved in a jar, nothing happens. Even the best quality apple seed will have no value if it does not bear fruits. It is only through nurturing the 'seed' with consistent, informed action that it goes through the stages of growth to its fullest blossoming. Whilst potentiality is a prerequisite, it is the becoming that has the utmost value.

The Universe is constantly showing us 'the way' through the principles operating in nature, but do we keep our minds open to receive? If we look at the above example, there are two aspects we may observe:

- A seed is valuable only when it blossoms to its fullest potential, i.e. its purpose.

- The fullest potential of a seed is valuable only when it creates value to others – it is not for itself.

Let us now integrate this observation into our own lives. If we plant a seed in the soil of our mind, we will need to carefully nurture the potential. Do we just randomly plant seeds? Do we carefully select those seeds that when it blossoms, create value for others? If we begin to nurture our potential self—give it love, care and understanding, be persistent and consistent in our efforts, never giving up on our purpose, having the patience knowing – just as much as you cannot force a seed to blossom into a fragrant rose within a few days – what you plant will mature in its own time, we are then in the process of value creation.

Unless you abandon it in the process, the seed will blossom.

Mind Seed

"You can have everything in life you want if you will just help other people get what they want." ~ Zig Ziglar Let us dig a little deeper before we plant this seed in our mind.

- Step one: When I found this idea, the seed, of this book, I checked to see what its quality was; the potential it had. How would the idea look in its fully manifested form? What purpose does it serve? Does it create value for the readers?

- Step two: Once I was convinced of the quality of the idea, the seed, I decided to implement it, i.e. plant it in the soil with the full preparation of tending to it to the best of my ability, through rain, hail or storm.

- Step three: After the idea was planted in the mind and nurtured through consistent action, the seed idea finally manifest into a book, which you are at this very moment holding in your hands. You have the power to decide what you want to do with it. It may fulfil its purpose by creating some value for you, or you may choose to ignore it.

Now it is not in my hands anymore.

You will note—whilst the first two steps are in your hands, the fruit is not. Whilst the seed and the action of nurturing lie in your hands, you decide what you choose to do with it, yet once the seed comes to fruition it is surrendered.

Surrender Your Control

"When you surrender and release the illusion of control, you begin to free-fall toward your destiny of a grand union with your original self..." ~ Byrant McGill

You may be wondering, after all the work done by us, why should not the fruit of our labour be in our hands? Why should I need to 'surrender' the fruit? Let us examine this further in three different instances:

- Situation one: If a man owning an orchard grows a thousand fruits. He decides to keep them all for himself and his family. But since they cannot consume so much the rest rot and go waste.

- Situation two: Suppose you were to write a book with great diligence and passion, but thereafter you want to keep it only for yourself. It does not reach out to others, and no value is created in anyone's lives. What purpose would the book serve?

- Situation three: A scientist makes a discovery and wants to keep the invention for himself and not share it with the world. His work would not only not add value to the planet but also not be available to future scientists to base their research and make further discoveries. For example, it is Einstein's work on energy and matter that has led to the modern-day understanding of quantum physics.

If you were to reflect on these situations, would it now make sense to say, when our work creates value for others, whether directly or indirectly, the more valuable it becomes? Giving out what you most want comes back to you better than you can imagine. If you want to create value in your life, then give value. The Law of Cause and Effect states that whatever you send into the universe comes right back manifold. Ralph Waldo Emerson called this 'The Law of Laws.' People usually start expecting from people for whom they have done something special, and spiral down into negativity when that person disappoints. The very thought of wanting a return or having expectations reinforce that your actions were not purely selfless. So do not be in any hurry to receive your goodies. Instead focus on the purity of your purpose, and the Universe will bring you the goodies, more than you can imagine, maybe not from those who you think owes you something, but from unexpected sources, in divine timing and in surprising ways.

Mind over Matter
The Story of Scott Harrison

When your mind overrules your circumstances, material limitations, and material cravings and works for the greater good, you not only up-level your personality, but your achievements have a far-reaching impact. Let us see the real-life story of Scott Harrison.

At twenty-eight years of age, Scott Harrison lived a decadent life, indulging endlessly in drugs, booze, and models. But a decade later, going through a 'dark night' of the soul, he asked himself a life-changing question, "What would the exact opposite of my life look like?" He wanted to completely turn his life around. In August 2004, Harrison quit his job as a night club and party promoter in Manhattan, New York City. He was inspired to apply for work at major non-profits. His partying background turned out to be a formidable obstacle in his path. However, Harrison was undeterred and his resolve unshaken. He persisted in his efforts until someone finally accepted his application. His voluntary services as a photojournalist were accepted for the Christian charity Mercy Ships, which operates a fleet of hospital ships offering free healthcare. He served aboard the *Anastasis*, which carried him to the coast of West Africa. The life-conditions that he saw there was a stark contrast to the life he had been living. This greatly overwhelmed Scott, and, in a span of thirteen months, he clicked over sixty thousand photographs. This was a life-changing experience for Scott.

Thoughts that empower you to change your own actions, is recognised as a true transformative force. Powerful thoughts which are consistent and potent can change the world.

Harrison founded Charity: water in 2006. At the time he had neither experience nor money. Today, his organisation has raised a few hundred million dollars to bring clean drinking water to more than eight million people worldwide. In his book, *Thirst* Harrison reveals the many road bumps and turns before Charity: water shaped up to become one of the most trusted and admired nonprofits in the world. He not only charts out how to build a better charity or a better business, but also shows how to have a better life, proving it's never too late to make a change.

Harrison is not only passionate about bringing clean water to everyone on the planet but also to change the way charity organisations operate. His organisation works on a hundred per cent donation model, and is committed to complete transparency. Charity: water has radically changed how social entrepreneurs work while inspiring millions of people to join its mission.

"It's one thing to idealise heroes. It is quite another to visualise yourself in their place. When I saw great people, I said to myself: I can be there." ~ Arnold Schwarzenegger

If you want to realise your dreams, you need positive thoughts that are not only persistent but also consistent enough to change your own actions. It is not about sitting around daydreaming, wishful thinking, or waiting for your dream life to be handed over to you in a platter.

In my work as a coach, I often find the new generation not satisfied with their lives. Some common complaints are, "I am not really sure why I get out of the bed in the morning" or "I am not fulfilled by the work that I am doing." The sad truth is that while your education may have prepared you well for getting a good job, for the most part, it has taught you nothing about how to realise your dream or how to live a fulfilling life. But even if you have spent years walking down a path that is crowded – comforted with the thought that you can't go wrong since others are doing the same thing, yet a part of you realises that what you are working at does not fulfil you – do not despair. You are about to discover how to uncover your purpose and bring your dream life into focus, and escape the trap of living life unfulfilled.

Are you willing to take the first step and commit to yourself wholeheartedly?

CHAPTER TWO

Living by Default

We either live with intention or exist by default.

Kirstin Armstrong

Are you living by default? For a large majority of people, we tend to slip into a default mode of living. A default life is one where you just passively accept life in whichever way events or circumstance show up for you. For a good part of my life, I was definitely living by default, was happily co-dependent and let others steer the boat for me—and it was no one's fault but my own! Until I woke up to the fact that it is a beautiful, magical world and it is for me to own it.

Que Sera Sera

"*Que sera sera*, whatever will be will be..." does this song play in your head? Are you resigned to whatever life throws your way? It's all too easy to fit into a routine of humdrum life and live by default. Day after day, one finds oneself repeating the same thing, which then turns into a yearly cycle. We look around us and see most people are doing the same thing, so we feel justified or safe.

A study in the UK suggests that 96% of people feel that they are living in autopilot mode. In an average lifetime, a quarter-million decisions we make are on autopilot. We do not have the awareness of the consequences of our thoughts, words, actions, or inactions which in reality moves us either towards or away from what we most want in our life. Then we feel life simply happens to us, blame it on fate, credit it on luck and so on.

Do you look at your life and feel that you don't have that special something that makes others appreciate you—no great achievement, talent, or recognition that you could be proud of. So you may have decided that special people are born special, or they are born with a silver spoon and are surely privileged. You, therefore, resign yourself to a life that happens to you. You wait for some excitement to pop into your life like a romance, a travel plan, a fun party, shopping binge, the next career break or promotion, the next accolade, a bigger car or house, or a windfall that takes care of your material desires. Pause a bit to think—is all this bringing in the happiness and fulfilment within you? You may even be an overachiever yet you wonder why true happiness or fulfilment eludes you. You have everything in your life, yet you experience this great discontent. There is one corner of you that knows and yearns for a life which holds more meaning and purpose.

Navigating the Eight Pillars of Life

Our life revolves around the following broad structures:

- Career or profession
- Family life
- Living environment
- Health and fitness
- Recreation and hobbies
- Friendships
- Community
- Religious or spiritual beliefs

Making a major change in just one of these areas will necessarily make a major change in the feel and quality of our day-to-day life. It simply can't, stay the same.

The eight broad structures are, more often than not, not decided consciously. The career you end up working in depends chiefly on what you saw as options when you graduated, at a time when you were only aware of a limited number of options. You went with whatever made sense at that time. As a result, what you may be doing today is most probably by default. You may be fortunate if you are already working in your niche, where you find most comfort and expansion. As humans, we are constantly evolving, so at twenty-one years of age, our priorities, expectations from life, awareness of ourselves can be quite different from what we grow into through our experiences and exposure. Many a time, we may want something different out of our life, but we keep running on the same track either out of habit, fear of change, or fear of perceived failure. So much of our lives consist of conditions we've fallen into. We gravitate unwittingly to what works in the short term. In other words, we seldom consciously decide how we are going to live our lives. We just end up living in certain ways.

When I work with my clients, I notice a few things in common. It is normal for almost everyone to have some kind of problem. An occasional tough spot does not appear as a problem when you view it as a challenge that you are willing to tackle. However, an issue that persists for years or decades, which becomes a theme in your life and also a part of your identity, becomes a considerable problem.

We as humans are programmed to seek pleasure and avoid pain. That often becomes the space from where we make our decisions. Long-term consequences escape our vision, and we end up looking only till the tip of our nose. So the choices we make are usually:

- simple to execute

- bring in short term gratification

- will not be time-consuming, difficult or tiring

- will be underwhelming

If even one of the eight areas of your life is causing significant pain or discontent, why wait to be thrown off the default track by a force of unforeseen events. Instead, introspect and make a conscious change. We often procrastinate till major upheavals force us into a different circumstance. An intentional change gives you a chance to see if your new situation resonates with you or not, and gives you a different perspective to the old one. If the new situation feels in alignment, then you're closer to finding what's right for you.

If it doesn't resonate with you, then you have a more clear understanding of what it is in your current life path that you like so much. You gain clarity on your values and goals, and you gravitate toward them more strongly. Your level of fulfilment and sense of peace with the world depend on how well-matched your values are to the life you're actually living.

By making a conscious change, a situation might get better, or it might get worse. You don't know until the change is made. This uncertainty is enough to keep most people from taking the step.

Would You Rather be Safe than Sorry?

"People have a hard time letting go of their suffering. Out of a fear of the unknown, they prefer suffering that is familiar." ~ Thich Nhat Hanh

When you live in the default mode, you feel stuck. It might feel like a song that plays on and on, stuck on the same groove. Initially, you may have liked it, but now it bores you or annoys you, and mostly doesn't serve to uplift you. Yet you have no idea how to play another song. A part of you wants to move forward, yet there is a part that holds back and resists the flow. There is a fear of the unknown – a fear of failure. Would you rather be in a safe place of familiarity, than take a chance and repent later?

We, humans, are programmed to fit into social mores. The simple route to take is to do what others have done or what others expect you to do. The need for love and acceptance is the most fundamental to man. Nathan Dewall, an American psychologist emphasises this fact by pointing out, "If you turn on the television set and watch any reality T.V program, most of them are about rejection and acceptance." As evident, the unpropitious twin of acceptance is rejection. Research has shown that rejection causes pain not only emotionally, but manifests into the physical reality as well. Man's survival instinct makes him stay away from anything that may cause pain. Abraham Maslow points out, "One can choose to go back toward safety or forward toward growth."

Abraham Maslow, an American psychologist, known for developing the *Hierarchy of Needs* – a theory of psychological health based on fulfilling innate human needs in priority, which eventually culminates in self-actualisation – explains that right after man's physiological needs, his need for safety forms the very basis of his world. According to Maslow, man can actualise his potential self only when his need for safety, love and acceptance, and self worth is met. This also explains why we inadvertently look for approval and validation from others. But if we are forced to take on the beliefs and goals of others, we often don't feel motivated enough. We look outside ourselves for remedies and solutions. When you live by default, you end up living a life which does not give you the most joy and fulfilment, instead it is a life built by avoiding negative situations and being passive. It is a recipe for mediocrity and following the 'herd' mind.

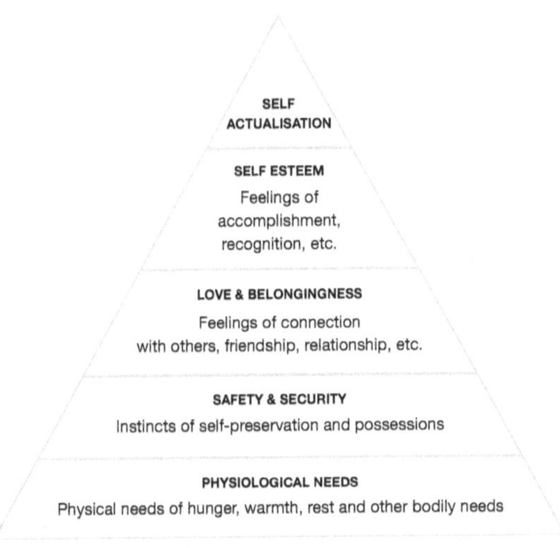

Figure 1. Abraham Maslow's hierarchy of needs: the lower 2 rung of the pyramid are the basic needs of man; the next 2 are the psychological needs of man; the apex of the pyramid depict the self-fulfillment needs of man where he strives to achieve his fullest potential and creative self-expression.

The Die is Not Cast

"If you plan on being anything less than what you are capable of being, you will probably be unhappy all the days of your life." ~ Abraham Maslow

It's all too easy to become a victim of your circumstances. But bear this in mind; your destiny is not set in stone. We easily forget that we are the ones who are truly in charge of our lives. If something shows up that does not serve your highest good, you have the power to change it. Do not form the idea that your life is not truly yours to create and give your power away to everyone and everything around you.

Are you prepared to leave your comfort zone and go forward towards growth?

CHAPTER THREE

You Can Design Your Life

Don't resist the truth of who you are; be your authentic self.

Many people and you may be one of them, feel a strong yearning for something more in Life. Questions may stir up within you, "What am I here to do?" and so on. Questions help you introspect and act as inner guidance that takes you towards your highest creative possibility. Suffocating that voice may cause you to feel stuck, bored, listless, blocked out of the flow, sad, depressed or frustrated. So it is important to pause, reflect and answer some of those questions, which can take your life to a new direction, where you feel more aligned to your authentic self, and live a life you truly want to live.

Where do You Begin?

You have a choice

First of all, it is important to realise that you have a choice. Your choices have compounded exponentially. You are the one who holds the driving wheel of your life and, once you realise that fully, you give yourself permission to grow, experiment, and begin designing the life of your dreams.

The first thing that we need to bring into our awareness is that whatever is showing up in our life right now is a result of choices that we have made in the past, whether intentionally or unintentionally. Likewise, whatever will show up in our life in the future are from the choices that we make right now.

What are you choosing?

- You choose to change the status quo because you feel you deserve better.

- If you experience discomfort in some aspects of your life, you choose to let go of the familiar and take a step towards the future you want.

- You choose not to allow change to intimidate you.

- You choose not to procrastinate for a later date.

- You choose not to force-fit into a life that your friend or your neighbour lives, simply because you believe theirs is better.

- You choose to design a life that fits you.

So the key to creating the future is the conscious choices we make in the NOW, whether in thoughts, words, or actions. Pay attention to the present.

Make yourself accountable

Once you realise that in this journey of life, you are the driver, take responsibility. This is because everything that shows up on the way is a result of your decisions. If you are the person behind the wheel, the route you undertake is your responsibility. If you take chances without the right preparation, you should be ready to take accountability for anything that goes amiss. When there is a fork in the road, you will need to decide which way to go, and you will need to take the onus. If you make yourself accountable, you will neither blame others or pass the buck to someone else, nor will you complain or whine about your bad luck. Instead, you will do your study and research and have the roadmap. You will develop your skills to scale heights and manoeuvre challenging terrains. Be a friendly accountability partner to yourself and not a harsh one. Don't be too self-critical. Do not beat yourself over a wrong turn. Just re-direct.

Above all, enjoy the journey!

Recognise that you are unique

Do you feel that you are unique? You may not think so but consider this: You are one amongst the billions of people inhabiting this planet, and nobody has lived the same story you have lived so far.

You are unique and talented in your own special way. Enjoy that uniqueness, as you weren't meant to be like someone else. You do not have to pretend to seem more like others. You do not have to hide the parts of you that you may feel are unacceptable, simply because they are different from the people you are comparing yourself with. Instead, embrace those differences to stand out.

You are gifted in a way no one else is—think of what makes you special.

Give yourself priority

Once you realise you've got choices, the next step is to give yourself priority. Spend a bit of time with yourself and figure out what you want your life to look like. Are you doing what you are doing to please significant people in your life? Are you merely doing things to meet others' expectations? Are you trying to follow a path that worked for someone else? Are you trying just to belong? Are you following a path simply because others told you so? You may be focused on supporting everybody else in your life and not think what is it you want your life to look like. I have done that myself for a long time and thought that it was normal. In case you are doing any of these, it is time to prioritise yourself.

Create a blueprint that specifies just what you want your life to look like. What do you want to spend your time doing; who all do you want around in your life; what do you want to create or achieve; how would you like to serve the community, society or the world; how would you take care of your financial and physical well-being without overlooking your deepest desire; how would your leisure hours look like.

Ask yourself some questions

- Why am I doing what I'm doing at present?

- If I continue doing what I'm doing, what kind of person will I become?

- What do I wish most to spend my time doing?

- What things would I rather do to support my physical, emotional, financial, and professional well-being?

- What completely absorbs my interest and attention?

- What are the things that light up my heart and soul? Are these present in my life right now?

- What is the last time that I engaged in an activity where I felt lit up from within and my energy activated?

- What holds me back from going for those things?

- Are there any practical impediments that prevent me from taking that path? Can those be overcome?

- Am I unsure about my gifts and doubt if I can share it with the world?

- What do I need to do to truly enjoy my work?

- What blocks me from moving forward?

- What is my authentic self, and how do I start moving toward my dream life?

- When is the last time I felt I was completely comfortable in my skin?

- Do I constantly have to adapt and try to please others to be accepted?

- Where and how will I end up if I continue to underutilise my strengths?

How you answer these above questions will lead you to a new direction in your life. Are you ready for the change?

Get ready for the change

Once you've figured out what you want your life to look like, it's time to set the ball rolling. Conditions are never perfect, so do not procrastinate anymore. For example, if you are planning to take a step towards a healthy lifestyle and kick the smoking addiction, check and see what really stops you? It's ok if the plan falls through a couple of times, but a wholehearted effort is what counts. Look at the underlying story that you're telling yourself, and make an effort to go past that.

"Quitting smoking can be a very good test of one's character. Pass the test, and you will have accomplished so much more than just get rid of one bad habit." ~ Abraham Maslow

Procrastination is an ailment that will take your dreams to its grave. Take action and start making the change a reality. Change is scary, but this should be scary in a very good way. The right time is always NOW.

Take small steps at a time

Begin with small steps. You can start making things happen by making small changes to your life's blueprint. As you gain momentum, you'll begin to experience significant growth in your life.

Let me give an example here. Your larger goal may be to become a professional dancer. The goals that help you reach there may be:

    a. become physically fit

    b. lose some weight

   c. join a class

   d. daily x hours of practice

   e. follow a disciplined lifestyle

So the smaller actionable steps you take here may be:

   a. locate a good class

   b. change your wake-sleep cycle

   c. start with walking 2 km every morning

   d. get help from a dietician to structure your diet or do-it-yourself (depending on what your financial priorities permit).

Whilst keeping your long-term goal in focus, start taking small actionable steps on the short-term ones.

Six steps to turn your life around:

1. Get out of your comfort zone.

2. Question and challenge your existing belief systems.

3. Act the way you would like to become in your life.

4. The bigger decisions you make should be heart-based, whilst the smaller ones from the head.

5. At no time take impulsive steps. Being under the sway of your emotions take you away from your goals and dreams.

6. Take professional help where ever needed.

Now step out in faith—faith in yourself, on your purpose, on the perfect unfolding in divine timing. Embrace that which you're passionate about, and get started on your amazing journey designing a life that reflects you perfectly. In a nutshell, life design involves the attempt on your part to design a life of your choice, whatever you wish your life to look like and feel. Prepare for the twists, and turns on your way, be flexible yet consistent and evolve to your ideal version.

Are you willing to hit the reset button and redesign your life?

CHAPTER FOUR

Change Begins with a Thought

*Your thoughts create your reality. Your mind is
more powerful than you know.*

Neale Donald Walsch

If we set out to create a life by choice, we need to understand the influence of thought and how to turn them around to serve our highest good, instead of being at the mercy of our 'monkey mind'. Thoughts are a form of energy and have the power to affect our physical reality.

Understand Your Thought

The original nature of the mind is to create thoughts. It is estimated that the mind creates anywhere between fifty thousand to eighty thousand thoughts per day. That sounds incredible—are we even aware of these many thoughts! If we are constantly consumed by our thoughts, it surely must consume a whole lot of our energy. Most of us do not think our thoughts consume energy. Try to remember a night in bed where you tossed and turned worrying about something. Have you wondered why even after the body rested for six hours or more you woke up feeling tired? Just as much as an overdose of physical activity can tire us, when our mind is burdened with thoughts, we feel tired and sapped of life force energy.

Dr. Marcus Raichle, an eminent neurologist, a recipient of the Kavli Prize for Neuroscience and a professor at Washington University School of Medicine, St. Louis says, "As an energy consumer, the brain is the most expensive organ we carry around with us." According to his research, on a typical day a person uses about 320 calories just to think.

Food for Thought

The fact that we are unaware of many of our thoughts, in a way reveals that most of them are simply redundant, and we can qualify them as 'waste' thoughts. If you bought a hundred apples and kept them in your fridge, could you have all of them? After some time, those apples would rot, and if you did not throw them away, they would stink. Even though apples are supposedly good for health, an excess of them is a waste. Likewise, excessive thoughts are also a waste—a waste of your mental energy.

There is another group of thoughts that we may qualify as 'poisonous'. Venomous thoughts of revenge, jealousy, hatred, hostility, pent-up anger, etc. poison our mind. What happens if we were to consume a poisonous fruit or stale or rotten food? When we consume poisonous thought, we literally fall ill. The mind-body connection is today a familiar idea. A growing body of research suggests that negative emotions and thoughts may have links to serious health problems. Poorly managed or repressed anger or hostility is also related to a host of health conditions, such as hypertension (high blood pressure), cardiovascular disease, digestive disorders, and infection.

Any form of negative thinking is harmful. Chronic stress can be created by negative attitudes and feelings of helplessness or hopelessness, which upsets the body's hormone balance. If you experience stress, you release cortisol, which has a variety of effects, including on the immune system. Science has now identified that stress shortens our telomeres—these are 'end caps' of our DNA strands that cause quicker aging. "Many negative emotions such as anger, fear, and frustration become problematic when those emotions turn into a more permanent disposition or a habitual outlook on the world," explains Emiliana Simon-Thomas, Ph.D., Science Director at the Greater Good Science Centre, UC Berkeley.

It's the Thought That Count

What kind of thoughts would you allow into your mind? Quantum physics reveals that there is an infinite number of possibilities out there. What you focus on is what will appear in your reality. If your thought is negative, then negative outcomes will manifest. On the other hand, if your thought and corresponding feeling is positive, the outcome that manifests is most certainly positive.

"The Law of Attraction says that like attracts like, and when you think and feel what you want to attract on the inside, the law will magnetise people, circumstances and events, to magnetise what you want." ~ Rhonda Byrne

Positive thinking is not about being in denial of reality. Psychologists have pointed out that positive thinking centres on such things as a belief in your abilities, a positive approach to challenges, and trying to make the most of the bad situations. It's natural for things not to go your way, many a time. Bad things may happen. Sometimes you will be disappointed or hurt by the actions of others. This does not mean that the world is out to get you or that all people will let you down, and you retreat into a shell or adopt a victim mindset. If you are a positive thinker, you will search for ways to improve the situation on the ground and try to learn from the experiences. Positive thinkers, therefore, have greater resilience and are more equipped to cope with stress, which in turn, leads to better cardiovascular health and higher immunity.

It is the thought that counts because everything that we say or do first originates in our mind as a thought. Wouldn't you say, it is highly unlikely a negative thought would give birth to a positive reality, or vice versa?

Got a Brainwave!

'A brainwave' can be a figure of speech to describe our thought, in a moment of newfound clarity, a shift in perspective, or an out-of-the-box idea. We've all experienced that magical feeling of being hit with a 'brainwave', which appears out of the blue perhaps during your morning walk, or whilst having your coffee, in your car to the office, or playing with your toddler.

But there is more to a brainwave than meets the eye. Neuroscientists and clinicians have been studying brainwaves for almost a century now. Brainwaves are produced by synchronised electrical pulses from masses of neurons communicating with each other and can be detected using sensors placed on the scalp. Brainwave speed is measured in Hertz (i.e. cycles per second), and they are divided into bands representing slow, moderate, and fast waves. The team at UK based Brainworks, founded by Christina Lavelle and Marty Wuttke have made a very interesting observation on their blog: "It is a handy analogy to think of brainwaves as musical notes—the low-frequency waves are like a deeply penetrating drum beat, while the higher frequency brainwaves are more like a subtle high pitched flute. Like a symphony, the higher and lower frequencies link and cohere with each other through harmonics."

A brainwave is a simple way to understand how our thoughts, emotions, and experiences may affect our physical reality.

- A deep restorative sleep produces delta waves. They are low-frequency sound waves which are slow and loud. They can be generated even during deep meditation.

- When our senses are withdrawn from external stimulus and turn within to a space of inner knowing or intuition theta waves are produced by our brain. Just when we drift off to sleep or moments before waking up, we are in the realm of Theta waves. That is where we access our subconscious, where we hold our fears, troubled experiences, and vulnerabilities.

- When our thoughts are calm and flow quietly, alpha waves are dominant. Alpha is the resting state for the brain when we are present to the moment, alert, relaxed, and in a flow state.

- Our normal waking state where we are engaged in problem-solving, judgment, decision making, or focused mental activity is dominated by beta waves. These waves become higher in frequency during complex problem solving, perceiving a threat, high anxiety, or excitement. Continual high-frequency processing takes an enormous amount of energy and tires the brain.

- Gamma waves are very subtle and high frequency. How gamma is generated yet remains a mystery to scientists. Researchers have discovered that it is highly active when in states of universal love, bliss, and in elevated states of virtues.

Once we understand how vital our thoughts are and how they can impact what we create in our lives, we will start paying attention to them.

Thoughts Become Things

"Thoughts become things. If you see it in your mind, you will hold it in your hand." ~ Bob Proctor.

We have seen how our thoughts and corresponding feeling create a brainwave of a particular frequency. You can also consciously choose to alter your frequency by practicing meditation, being in nature, or immersing in a creative process. You will find people are increasingly practicing meditation all over the world. This is because we want to shift our state from the harmful effects of high-frequency beta waves to a calmer state.

Meditation helps slow down the brainwave frequency to alpha, theta, and even delta.

Thoughts are forms, and when thoughts are infused with feelings, they gain substance to materialise into our world. Thoughts are inherently either love-based or fear-based. Thoughts that are fuelled by fear-based emotions giving rise to insecurities, anxiety, dissatisfaction, anger, and hate or being overly critical, will 'become' a reality which we experience as negative. The outcomes may be unfortunate, bad, unbearable, etc.

On the other hand, thoughts that are nurtured by love-based emotions like gratitude, acceptance, appreciation, compassion, generosity, peace, and goodwill shall create a reality which we experience as positive. Such outcomes are good, fortunate, happy, pleasant, etc.

Let us take the thought-form of 'money'. Some people may be subconsciously or even consciously programmed to feel.

- Money is the root of all evil.

- It's a struggle to make money.

- There is never enough money.

- Only a privileged few have lots of money.

- One easily runs out of money.

The above fear-based belief systems that a person may hold will generate similar feelings. When we infuse the thought-form of 'money' with such fear-based feelings, we will create a reality where we will never be comfortable around 'money'. Our relationship with money will remain unhealthy. We might reject money if we feel 'it's the root of all evil'. We will be anxious and stressed if we feel 'it's a struggle to make money'. Even when we earn well we may still suffer from a feeling of lack since we've decided 'there is never enough money'. We may want to hoard or be miserly if we feel 'money runs out easily'. We may not even try to better our circumstances if we feel 'only a privileged few have lots of money'. So on and so forth...

On the other hand, if we infuse the thought-form of 'money' with feelings of gratitude, respect, acceptance, generosity, or well-being, then we create a good experience in reality around that thought-form. The probabilities, of money flowing to us effortlessly and easily, are much higher.

To summarise how our thoughts become our destiny:

- Our beliefs influence our thoughts.

- Our thoughts generate our feelings.

- Our feelings determine our attitude.

- Our attitude influences our action.

- Our actions create our destiny.

Are you willing to look at your beliefs,

question their relevance, check if they have a positive or a negative influence on your thoughts and if negative are you willing and determined to change them?

CHAPTER FIVE

Define Your Success

Success is being able to effectively carry out and complete what you have set out to do and enjoying the process of growth towards your highest potential.

To me, success is subjective and personal. You're the only one who gets to decide what it looks like for you, and you're the only one who can make it a reality. I would like to invite my readers to discover their idea of success, instead of simply accepting the idea as given by others, and re-evaluate if necessary.

Success Looks Different to Different People

"Work is that which you dislike doing but perform for the sake of external rewards. At school, this takes the form of grades. In society, it means money, status, privilege."~ Abraham Maslow

Around the world, people hold various views of what success is and how to achieve it. For Anita, a middle school student, success could mean good grades and topping her class. For Saif, success could mean graduating from high school and getting admission into an Ivy League college. For Bill, it could mean accolades and trophies. In your years as a student and in your years of youth, much of the attention, time, energy, and effort go in the pursuit of success. When students prepare for national-level exams, it is as though their life is on the line, so much so that some parents are as jittery as their child. But do the marks really define our value or the measure of our success? That can be very discouraging for students who have not scored the desired marks despite putting in their best efforts, or even lose hope if they view it as a failure.

To a corporate executive success could mean invitations to corporate events, business class travel to exotic destinations, wining and dining in Michelin star restaurants, and a second home on the beach. But their success can also look like a 12x7 work week, constantly on-call, no quality time with family, postponed vacations.

Success can mean many things to different people. For some, it could be having abundant wealth, finding their soul mate, marrying and having adorable kids, working for a social or environmental cause, and making a difference to the planet. For others, it might mean being appreciated and recognised for their talent be it in music, arts, theatre, sports, or any other field. Some could feel success is climbing the corporate ladder, beating others to the competition, while some other might believe having a steady job and having a contented family life is the measure of success.

Are you chasing a stressful version of success and your dream job doesn't seem to fit into your dream anymore? It is important to check if you are merely working to gain money, status, and privilege, or are you following your passion to bring forth your highest potential, which impacts your environment (family, society, environment, country or world) in a positive way. This is what will bring fulfilment to you. There is a difference between achievement and holistic success.

What is Your Motivation?

The Maslow motivation theory is one of the most influential theories on needs motivation (refer to figure1. in page 22). According to Abraham Maslow's theory, human needs have been categorised into five basic kinds: physiological, safety and security, belongingness, self-esteem, and self-actualization. The other two theories that are also significant in workplace motivation are Alderfer's theory, where he categorizes broadly into Existential, Relatedness and Growth needs, whilst in McClelland's theory we have the Need for Affiliation, Need for Power and Need for Achievement. You may observe – whilst in Maslow's and Alderfer's theories, needs can be broadly categorized into lower order needs and higher order needs, McClelland talks only of the higher order needs. What has evolved from these observations and theories are the six basic human needs, which are usually targeted in neuro-linguistic programming (NLP) techniques.

The Six Basic Human Needs

- Certainty

- Love and connection

- Variety

- Significance

- Growth

- Contribution

The need for certainty corresponds to the 'need for safety and security' which is the second from the base of Maslow's hierarchy of needs pyramid. Any person, whose need for certainty is dominant, will give importance to factors of stability—be it in a job or relationship and even where he lives. If your need for certainty is high you might be reluctant to try new dishes in a new restaurant; you will prefer to go to the same departmental store to shop even when new ones are coming up in the neighbourhood; you might not like to change your car for a new one from a different stable; you might prefer to live in a familiar place and resist making any changes.

For a person whose need for certainty is dominant, it might not be a great idea to start a business just because his friends, parents, or spouse urges him to. This can make him very uncomfortable, so in such a condition success would be unlikely. You need to enjoy what you do in order to be committed to it.

One must keep in mind that these needs are not fixed or cast in stone. Over the years, as we evolve, our predominant need also changes. So it is important to base your decisions on what predominates at the current time.

The need for variety is inversely related to the need for certainty. If your need for variety is dominant, you will love to experience different things in life, try new cuisines, different fashion, a variety of entertainment, several hobbies or interact with people having varied interests. You might feel stifled if you are compelled to be an environment where you are required to do the same mundane things or live in a place which is not buzzing with life or where access to a variety of things is not there.

The need for love and connection corresponds to 'love and belonging' which is the third from the base of Maslow's pyramid. If your need for love and connection is dominant, you might not be happy in purely mind-based activities or if you have to work in isolation. You should rather opt for working in areas which call for networking, or work in a team or be part of group-based activities. In most likelihood, you will thrive doing a heart-based job or if you follow your passion. If your need for love and connection is high, you might not feel wholly fulfilled if, you work as a stockbroker, investment banker or structured product analyst merely for the sake of the good money you make.

The need for significance corresponds to 'esteem' which is the second-highest in Maslow's hierarchy of needs. For anyone whose need for significance is dominant, fulfilment comes from being in leadership roles or taking centre stage. They need to play a bigger role in life and be admired for what they do. If your need for significance is dominant, you might be more comfortable being an entrepreneur rather than taking orders from others. You may not care much for the hardship that might come with a start-up as long as you play a significant role.

The need for growth and the need for contribution corresponds to 'self-actualisation' which is at the apex of Maslow's hierarchy of needs pyramid. As an individual evolves toward self-actualisation, any activity towards self-development will bring him fulfilment more than any material benefits. Such a person welcomes challenges and experiences that will be favourable to his growth. He will welcome wealth and abundance, but his primary motivation is self-development and growth. When a person grows significantly, he will be hugely motivated to be contributing to humanity.

Before you design your life, you need to take an unbiased look into what 'need' predominates in you. You may even rank the 'needs' according to their order of importance to you. Your need is your biggest motivation, so taking action accordingly will bring you a measure of success.

Through the Lens of Human Needs
The Story of Bill Gates

Let us study the motivation that powered software luminary Bill Gates from being a Harvard dropout to become America's wealthiest business magnet, holding the Forbes title of the richest person in the world from 1995–2017.

Love and Connection: The need for love and connection is not necessarily restricted to romantic connection—it is just one aspect of it. The need for love and connection is a universal need. It can manifest through following one's passion or heart's calling;

doing things from the heart; or pursuing a heart-based activity.

Gate's heart's calling, was computers, and he sincerely followed his passion with dedication and determination right from childhood. Gates wrote his first software program when he was in the eighth grade.

Microsoft co-founder Paul Allen in his memoir *Idea Man* reveals some amazing stories about his friend Bill Gates, and how their friendship started off with writing software codes. This soon turned into a small business venture after the duo, along with programmer Paul Gilbert, developed the program Traf-O-Data, which even earned them twenty thousand dollars.

Significance: Apart from his passion for computers, Gates had clear ideas of his own and was not one to join the herd. Although he joined Harvard to pursue Law, he continued to follow his interest and passion for computers. He had high self-belief, and nothing deterred him from his pursuit. Gates dropped out of Harvard when he saw the opportunity to start his own computer software company along with his longstanding friend and partner Paul Allen. Together they launched Microsoft in 1975, which became the world's largest software for personal computers.

Growth: The next 30 years of his life, Gate's growth was phenomenal. He was listed as a billionaire in *Forbes* in 1997, and the following year he was ranked number one in the 'Top 50 Cyber Elite' by *Time*. Gates was the world's youngest self-made billionaire with a worth of one and half million dollars, and he held the top spot on the list of 'The World's Billionaires'

18 times. Gates was undoubtedly one of the most influential men of the twenty-first century and won innumerable awards, accolades, and several prestigious titles were conferred on him.

Contribution: Motivated by his need for contribution Gates in 1994 formed the William H. Gates Foundation. A few years later, together with his wife, Gates not only went ahead forming the charitable Bill and Melinda Gates Foundation in 2000, he also provided personal donations to several educational institutions. In the year, 2006, Gates announced that he would transition out of his routine roles in the company by 2008, so that he could devote more time to philanthropy. In yet another significant act of philanthropy Bill and Melinda Gates along with investor Warren Buffett each signed a commitment they called the 'Giving Pledge' where they each pledged to donate at least half of their wealth, over the course of time, to charity.

It is evident that when an individual pursues heart-based goals and dreams, he evolves from his basic needs. It is man's higher needs of significance and growth that propel him towards self-actualisation, which subsequently motivates him to make significant contributions to society and humanity at large.

Tangible vs Intangible

We have got conditioned to regard achieving only tangible goals as success. Things that are quantifiable, for example, the money in our bank, the number of friends we have, the degrees we hold, our position at work, the cars we drive, the houses we have, the brands we wear, among many such parameters. Do we set goals on the kind of relationships we have, our self-development and growth through learning, our contribution to society, our virtues, or how much fulfilment, happiness or peace we have in our lives? Does success depend upon what others perceive of me, or what I experience in my life? For transformative success, we need to value the intangible.

Gross National Happiness
The Story of King Jigme Singye Wangchuk

The 4th King of Bhutan, King Jigme Singye Wangchuck, ascended to the throne at 17 years of age. On a trip through India soon after his ascension, he was asked by an Indian journalist about the GDP of his country. The king's reply to this question was historic and made thought leaders of the world sit up and also piqued the interest of the United Nations. He said, "Why are we so obsessed with Gross Domestic Product, why don't we care about Gross National Happiness?"

The phrase Gross National Happiness (GNH) was first coined by the young king of Bhutan, who realised that a more holistic approach was needed for sustainable development and progress. He, therefore, gave equal importance, to intangible non-economic factors like happiness and mental well-being. This has influenced Bhutan's economic and social policy, and also captured the imagination of others far beyond its borders and influenced places like the United States, Canada, Thailand, and Finland.

The king was talking about an alternative role model of success. GNH Index includes both the usual socio-economic concerns such as health, education, and living standards, as well as lesser considered aspects such as culture and psychological well-being.

The Bhutanese government aims to create the conditions for happiness and the general well-being of their population, rather than a subjective psychological ranking of 'happiness'. For this purpose, they have created a measurement tool that would be useful for policymaking based on four essential pillars, nine key indicators, and seventy two different matrixes.

What is quite significant is the fact, Bhutan turned from Absolute Monarchy to Constitutional Monarchy without a coup or bloodshed, and subsequently, Bhutan became a Democracy and had its first official elections in 2007.

A Toast to Your Success

For holistic success in life, a balance between the tangible and intangible aspects of life is essential. The following *eight* steps can act as a guideline:

1. Identify your passion and find the courage to follow it. This may not be too easy for many. It's easy to fall into a routine that leaves you bored or unfulfilled. Even though you are ready to make the switch, but you're not sure how to. I personally think a regular practice

of mindfulness meditation is very beneficial and is a great way to begin.

2. Visualise with clarity on your long-term goal. The goal should be in sync with the aspects of your life, which are important to you. It should include things that bring you joy and eliminate situations that cause undue stress and discomfort. Align with your dominant need and be authentic to your truth.

3. Focus on the long-term goal, but create small milestones that take you towards it. Celebrate (make a fun ritual for yourself) when you reach every small milestone. Never take your eye off the focus.

4. Remove distractions that take you away from your target. Indulging in too many sensory inputs create undue distractions. That will lure you off your track, and much of productive energy is lost.

5. Consistent effort is the key: If you have identified your passion, you will enjoy the journey even when you face roadblocks. You will not be sidetracked by turmoil as you will understand it is temporary and you will make the effort to work your way around it.

6. Be open to ideas: a) Listen and learn b) Observe and absorb c) follow your curiosity d) ask relevant questions e) don't hesitate to take help e) connect with people.

7. Be persistent even in the face of adverse situations.

8. Serve the greater good, because you cannot be successful if the only person you serve is yourself. I have talked about this at length in the first chapter. Assuming you have read it, you will surely understand the value of serving.

How does success look to you? Are you ready to commit to a life of purpose? Re-define your success by aligning to your authentic self.

CHAPTER SIX

The Subconscious Can Block Your Success

The major problem is that people are aware of their conscious beliefs and behaviours, but not of subconscious beliefs and behaviours. Most people don't even acknowledge that their subconscious mind is at play when the fact is that the subconscious mind is a million times more powerful than the conscious mind and that we operate 95 to 99 percent of our lives from subconscious programs.

Bruce Lipton

We all want to create a life that is joyful, purposeful, abundant, and fulfilled. A life filled with moments of wonder and made more meaningful with loving relationships. But unfortunately, in the course of our lives, we are led to believe that a life like this would be utopia and can only exist in daydreams. You may be wondering why after reading all those personal development books, chanting magical mantras, doing *yogaasanas,* and attending popular personal development courses, you still can't seem to create the life of your dreams. Do not be discouraged, because you are on the right track. What you seek, you will surely find.

The Subconscious Mind Can Block Your Success

What most people are not aware of is that your subconscious mind is a very powerful and compelling force that might hold you back in life preventing you from moving in the direction of your dreams, goals, and intentions. Those hidden subconscious, self-limiting blocks, negative thoughts, feelings, and emotions were largely formed in your mind before the age of six.

We all like to believe that we are in control of our destiny—if we just work hard enough and have clear goals, we can reach our dreams. In fact, there might be times where you feel you've reached the end of the road or like you've hit a brick wall. Perhaps everything you're doing just isn't working right. You might be feeling stuck in the same place unable to move towards your dream life. This might lead you to wonder, "Am

I doing something wrong?" Don't need to fret. You're probably not doing anything wrong. You just need to dig deeper.

Your Hidden Blocks to Success

We all have blocks to success that aren't obvious at all. For the powerful force of your subconscious to work with you, and for you, rather than against you, you first need to understand these hidden blocks that may be sabotaging your happiness and even your progress.

Childhood Conditioning

The limiting mental constructs that we all cling to so dearly, which cause so much pain and sadness, are largely a result of what happened to us as a child. Mostly everything that people have been conditioned to stems from the initial response of childhood. This primarily comes from our immediate envionment. Ideally a child is supposed to be taken care of and honoured as living humans who are meant to feel safe, be able to express honestly and encouraged to discover themselves.

The problem arises because most parents and guardians of children have already formulated in their minds the purpose of the child, thus limiting the child's scope to manoeuvre and navigate their own life. A parent or guardian might feel they are doing everything in the child's interest even if it goes completely against the child and all of their truth. When a person is denied their truth, their ability to express themselves becomes limited, creating a poison of discontent and suppression within their system, which over time leads to sickness, disease, and suffering of the mind and body.

Limiting Beliefs

We all have core beliefs that guide the decisions we make. They affect how we interpret the events in our lives and therefore influence the way we think, feel, and behave. Whilst acknowledging our core beliefs, it is important to examine which ones might be inaccurate, unproductive, and limit our potential. Limiting beliefs constrain us in some way or the other. Just by believing them, we limit our possibilities. They are either about us or our self-identity; they may be about others, or they may be about the world in general. Often these beliefs are wedged so much in our subconscious mind and have become so much a part of our personality that it becomes difficult to dislodge them. It is important to identify those beliefs that are making you less effective and sabotaging your best efforts.

A few common limiting beliefs are:

- I cannot be my real self, or I will be judged.

- I cannot ask for what I want; I might get rejected.

- It's selfish of me to want more.

- If I trust someone, they might break my trust.

- If I give away my heart, it might get broken.

- I am too old to pursue my dreams.

- What if I try and fail.

- I am not smart enough.

- I am not educated enough.

- You can succeed only if you work very hard.

- You can make money if you have money.

- Money does not grow on trees.

Does one of the above limiting beliefs resonate more strongly with you over the others? Which area of life would you most like to impact right now? Now try to see, what is the correlation between the belief you hold and the challenge that you face, which holds you back from getting what you want? For example, your self-limiting belief can be an obstacle to hitting your weight-loss goals, making more money, or feeling more love and connection. Becoming conscious of these beliefs is the first step towards reaching your goals, dreams, and desires.

Whilst in this chapter I will present some of these inner hurdles, in the following chapter you will find guidelines about how to overcome them.

Negative Self Talk

Another form of the self-destructive pattern is negative self-talk. Negative self-talk is an inner dialogue you have with yourself that limits your ability to believe in yourself and your abilities to reach your potential. So when you have a retrogressive thought – where you question your ability to make positive changes in your life, or your confidence in your ability to do so – it significantly diminishes you. Because of this, negative self-talk is not only stressful but also a hindrance to your success. Any pattern of talk that begins with the following prelude invariably pushes you back.

- I cannot do this...
- I am not able to...
- I am not smart enough to...
- I always...
- I should not have done...
- I am not capable...
- Nothing good happens...
- If only I were...
- What if...

Check and see how frequently you talk this way. When you know what causes you harm, it is not so difficult to change your subconscious patterns.

Lack of Self Love

Very often, we are driven by a desire to excel and do everything right, so we end up being too hard on ourselves. There is this persecutory inner voice that constantly tells us how we could have done things better. From being late to a dinner party to dropping a file on the floor, or spilling coffee on our shirt, we are often overcritical with ourselves and have developed an unconscious reflex to put our self down for every little thing, no matter how ridiculous or insignificant.

Many studies in psychology reveal self-love and self-compassion are the keys to holistic well-being. In his book *Self-Compassion: The Proven Power of Being Kind to Yourself*, Dr. Kristin Neff writes, "Love, connection, and acceptance are your birthright."

What is self-love? According to some, it refers to our ability to hold ourselves in esteem and have confidence in our worth, no matter what happens around us. Self-compassion and self-love are often used interchangeably. It is the ability to be kind to oneself and treating oneself with understanding and forgiveness. It is the acknowledgment that people are not perfect and that personal experiences are part of the larger human experience. It is the emotional stability that comes with not over-identifying with painful emotions.

The level of our self-love affects every aspect of our life. The way we feel about ourselves impacts our career, relationships, how much money we make, how truly happy we are, and our perception of the world as well as others' perception of us. Having more self-love builds resilience in the face of adversity. This enables people to recover more quickly from trauma or romantic separation and help us cope with failure or embarrassment more easily.

Lack of self-love disconnects us from our true authentic self. This can lead to a person being more reactive or having relationship issues. It can cause anxiety, diffidence, and even depression. When our sense of self-worth is diminished, the subconscious will block anything worthy from coming your way. Since the ego projects everything outside of itself we tend to desire respect and love from others without giving it to ourselves first. What we fail to realise is that we are expecting others to give us what they too have not developed for themselves.

The questions below will reveal to you your level of self-love.

- Do you believe your self-worth depends on how people feel about you?

- How many times have you put other people's dreams and desires ahead of your own?

- When you make a mistake, do you beat yourself up?

- Do you feel guilty about taking care of yourself or doing things for yourself?

If your answer is in the affirmative for most of the above, you need to retrain your mind by practicing self-compassion and self-love. Over time, you will not need validation from others and begin to feel more comfortable in your own skin, accepting yourself just the way you are. When we are aligned with our truth with courage and compassion, we will find joy, happiness, and open our hearts to living our purpose.

These blocks that are often hidden in our subconscious mind will manifest in our lives in the form of doubt, fear, and worry or anxiety, which is our biggest hindrance to living a life which we would love to live.

The Faces of Fear

Fear in any shape or form holds us back from living a life by choice. In case any of the following fears resonate with you, then you will need to look into the subconscious blocks discussed above, to identify where does the fear originate.

- You may fear what people around you might think or say if you take a step in a direction that doesn't match with the expectations of your family or the culture you are a part of.

- You may fear to fail in your attempts to move towards a bigger vision, so you rather not try.

- You may have fear of the unknown, so you rather remain within familiar boundaries and be afraid of stepping out.

- You may have fear of other people's judgments or fear of annoying others.

Whatever they may be, fear contracts your heart and hinders you from living your best life. Very aptly expressed by the author of the *Harry Potter* series, J.

K. Rowling, "It is impossible to live without failing at something, unless you live so cautiously that you might as well not have lived at all, in which case you have failed by default."

Doubt Fires

We are often triggered by various doubts which either prevent us from following our intuitive calling or might stop us dead on our tracks even if we are moving in that direction.

- You may doubt your capabilities, to begin with.

- You may even doubt the effectiveness of your goals.

- You may have doubts about whether the reward after all your efforts will be worthwhile enough.

- You may be in doubt of the advice you receive.

- You might even doubt the possibility of a happy and peaceful life.

- You may doubt finding the right partner.

- You might doubt the fact that it is possible to find fulfilment in all the aspects of life that mean a lot to you.

Woesome Worries

Although some of our worries might be existential, we more often tend to worry over inconsequential things.

We have told ourselves that it is normal to worry. Have you ever wondered what makes you worry?

- We feel worried whenever we anticipate a negative outcome which is beyond our control. For example, we get worried if we see a cloudy sky on a day we have planned an outdoor party.

- We worry when we imagine the worst case scenario. For example, you have made a serious mistake at work, and you imagine the worst possible fall out, maybe even lose your job.

- We feel worried when we do not see the desired expectation being met or there is a delay in gratification. For example, you are expecting a promotion, but you are still waiting for confirmation, whereas your colleague has already received a hike.

- We get extremely worried when we imagine something going wrong, and we do not have the information. For example, your boyfriend has not replied to your message, which he typically does promptly and you start feeling insecure, or your child has not returned home from a party much beyond the acceptable time, and you imagine all kinds of negative things that could have happened.

- If we are a perfectionist, we might get worried over every single detail that does not turn out to be just the way we want it to be.

- We might have existential worries like how to pay our bills, how to take care of an ailing family member with our limited resources, and so on.

When you worry it depletes you of the much needed positive energy that is needed to handle the situation or problem. When you are enmeshed in worry it distorts the reality and everything appears much worse. As a result, the action that needs to be taken in the present is lost in the distraction of unwanted emotions. Worry can also be due to our apprehension of events that might not actually happen, causing you unnecessary torment, which leave you feeling more burdened than you really are.

Check to see if your worry is based in truth and there is a valid reason for this worry. If yes then identify a small, practical step you can take to conquer this worry. Conquering worry makes it possible to strive for progress over perfection and truly live a life of freedom.

Your subconscious can only work with what it has been fed with since childhood and whatever input it receives through the senses as well as through the conscious mind. If due to external influence, ignorance or neglect, your subconscious resonates with a number of limiting beliefs about any area of your life (i.e. career, money, relationships, health, etc.), then no matter your level of effort or how strong your intention to achieve your goal, you are likely to get stuck down the line.

Knowing and understanding your subconscious beliefs and patterns is crucial in achieving success.

Have you identified your limiting beliefs and repeating life patterns? Are you willing to look objectively and identify them with courage and honesty?

CHAPTER SEVEN

Uncover Your Hidden Blocks

Your subconscious influences your attitude and actions and gives you insights and solutions. To understand how yours influences you, become more conscious of your subconscious.

In the previous chapter, we have seen how the patterns that are held in our subconscious mind, the pre-programmed ideas and limiting beliefs that are imprinted there may be sabotaging our best intentions. Even when we take pride in our independent ideas, opinions, or actions, in reality, they may be just automated responses from our subconscious. That is why we often repent our impulsive words or action. Unknowingly we are merely slaves to our subconscious mind. The nature and function of the subconscious are to attract circumstances and situations from the outer matrix of our reality, according to the imprints it holds within. We may now understand how powerful our subconscious mind is. So why not make it our friend and ally!

To become more aware of the hidden patterns, you need to look objectively at your life. For this, you must be completely unbiased, courageous, and honest. This is not as easy to do as it might appear initially. Would you be willing to admit that perhaps the reason you do not see results in a certain area of your life has nothing to do with others? We all tend to look for a scapegoat for our problems in life and absolve ourselves of any responsibility. This may not be completely your fault. The fact is that you may know no better. When we want an aspect of our life to go a certain way, but despite our efforts, we are unable to turn things around, we then tend to feel helpless. We need to find the reason for why this is happening, and due to our inability to grasp the situation, we turn to our outside reality and hold other people or circumstances to be responsible for our plight. Even though it might be hard to accept, but the fact is that it has everything to do with us.

Through the Looking Glass

Whatever is happening in our external life is but a reflection of what is happening inside of you.

You are the one who determines what inner patterns you will hold and therefore, what vibe you will exude. As we saw in Chapter Four, different thoughts have different frequencies, and that is what determines our vibration. Our life on the outside will always reflect the patterns of subconscious beliefs and thoughts. We are so preoccupied either in conducting our routine life or in succeeding and doing all the right things that using our life as a mirror to the subconscious just does not occur to us.

Take a look at what is showing up in your life and use that as a mirror. Let us take an example: What is showing up for you in your life right now that makes you unhappy? If it is unhappy relationships, then chances are that your relationship with yourself is not a happy one. You may ask yourself the following questions:

- What expectations do you have of yourself?

- If you don't come up to your expectations, what do you feel about yourself?

- Are you too harsh on yourself?

- Do you accept yourself as you are, or do you beat yourself up over your shortcomings?

- When you disappoint yourself, do you encourage or disparage yourself?

- Do you wish you were like someone else?

If your answer to at least three of the above is in the affirmative, then you need to look into your subconscious blocks of self-love and acceptance. Likewise, take any area of your life you would like to improve and look objectively at the reflection. Know that it is your looking glass and ask yourself pertinent questions that can help uncover your hidden beliefs.

In a radio interview with Barnet and Freeman, Law of Attraction Coach Joe Vitale says, "The whole life is the mirror of my consciousness. If I don't like something that I see in the mirror, I don't go and fracture the mirror, or change the mirror... I look at me because I am the projector."

Uncovering your subconscious blockages is the first step towards emotional freedom and getting success in whichever area of your life you wish to. In the previous chapter, we have discussed the hidden blocks to success. Now let us see how we can overcome these blocks.

Stop Negative Self-Talk

Awareness, as always, is the first step. You need to understand that negative self-talk is not the truth;

rather it reflects your negative beliefs and feelings about yourself. These are your perceived shortcomings that could have originated in childhood and your growing-up days. If you can recognise your self-talk as nothing more than baggage from your past that you are unnecessarily lugging around, you can then choose to gradually shift your way of thinking. When you catch yourself slipping into your old habit of belittling or de-motivating yourself, you can do the following:

Reframe

You simply need to frame or express the words you usually tell yourself repeatedly, in a different manner. Try to be positive as well as authentic. Here are a few examples:

Self-talk: "I can't do anything well."

Reframe: "I CAN do anything I set my mind on."

Self-talk: "I am too old to start a new venture."

Reframe: "I am only 40. Colonel Sanders began Kentucky Fried Chicken at age 65."

Reframes help put things in perspective. If you do this repeatedly, you will find that gradually your negative self-talk is dying out. Also, you will gain more clarity about your situation.

Affirmations

Affirmations are words or thoughts that assert, proclaim, or declare something. Negative self-talk makes you feel small, incapable, and stuck, whereas positive affirmations can act as an antidote and help you move forward with encouraging assertions. Once you realise the negative thoughts that go through your head, use affirmations to change it. Here are a few examples:

Self-talk: "My sister is better than me. Everyone loves her."

Affirmation: "I am good enough... I am worthy of love."

Self-talk: "I don't think I can do it."

Affirmation: "Of course I can do it. I am getting better at it every day."

Affirmations thrive on reiterations and they in time create new neural pathways bringing in a change to your existing thought patterns, which are self-deprecating. Affirmations if done in the right manner can help you change your reality and live your dream.

Practice Self Love

Psychology studies have revealed that self-love and compassion are the keys to mental health and well-being. It helps a person to have more resilience when faced with adversity or even embarrassing situations, and cope well with trauma or failure. Self-love builds a healthy sense of self-worth, which in turn keeps us healthy, both mentally and physically. You can start cultivating some self-love right away.

- Be warm and understanding to yourself when you suffer, fail, or feel inadequate.

- Be kind to yourself. treat yourself with understanding and be ready to forgive yourself for any mistake committed. Just take the learning from any situation and do not punish yourself unnecessarily.

- Stop over-identifying with painful emotions and hold yourself responsible for everything. Painful emotions are like a burning coal; if you hold on it will burn you. Learn to let go.

- Try not to be a perfectionist. Studies show that perfectionists are at a higher risk of several illnesses. Acknowledge that people are not perfect, and "To err is human". Our personal experiences are a part of the larger human experience. It is important to understand that our frailties are a stepping stone to our growth.

- Self-compassion can free us from the grip of self-criticism, so be mindful each time you are too harsh with yourself.

- Practice affirmations in order to raise your sense of self-worth.

- Meditate 15 minutes every day and connect to the essence of who you are.

At the very core, we have a deep capacity to love, experience joy, and compassion. When we are disconnected from the Source, we lose sight of our intrinsic self. We start identifying what we are rather than who we are. Our identities come from external sources; for example what race, religion, culture or sex we belong to, what work we do, what position we hold, what qualifications and accolades we have gathered, how we look and what possessions we have. We seldom value ourselves for what we feel, how we connect or relate to others, what are our inner gifts, and how they serve others, how rich we feel inside. When we are connected to our authentic self, we can embrace and accept ourselves just the way we are, and not be misguided by appearances or misdirected by others' thoughts and opinions of us.

Remove Your Abundance Blocks

"Like the air you breathe, abundance in all things is available to you. Your life will simply be as good as you allow it to be." ~ Abraham-Hicks

What does abundance look like to you? Does it mean being a millionaire, and having the best things in life? Does it mean having what makes your soul sing—having more love and connection, having financial, emotional and physical freedom, being loved and valued by the person you love, making a living by doing the work that you feel passionate about, feeling the joyousness that comes with fulfilment and abundance?

Your subconscious mind does not distinguish between true or false. It doesn't make judgments or form an opinion. So you can methodically imprint beliefs that are in harmony with your goals, and once these beliefs are accepted by the subconscious, they will work within you to create the reality you desire. The subconscious mind simply takes what is believed to be true. In the case of self-talk, this would be positive reinforcements about having a life you would love. You first mentally design for yourself, imagining all the nitty-gritty details that you would like to see in your life. What you feel intensely the subconscious believes it to be true. In turn, this 'truth' is compounded and reinforced in your internal beliefs, which will attract you those positive results.

Doing the following can certainly help, so try them out for yourself:

- Change your feelings: When you are feeling down, ask yourself what are the thoughts that led you to feel this way? At that point, you can change your thoughts. And when you change your thoughts, you change the way you feel, and only then can you change your life experience.

- Open your heart to receiving: Learn how to be happy receiving from others. Open your heart to compliments and know that you deserve them. Welcome help that comes to you willingly, and also know that you deserve being cared for. Be happy with little gifts, hugs, appreciation, a warm smile, and know that you are loved.

- Practice gratitude: Gratitude is a wonderful way to attract abundance your way. Make gratitude your new habit: you can have a little gratitude journal where at the end of each day you can write all the things you feel good about. You can express your gratitude for a beautiful sunrise, a flower blooming in your backyard, an old friend calling you up to enquire. Make it a point to write down ten "thank you" sentences every day. In the beginning, it might be difficult, but soon you will love it.

- Abundance affirmations: Affirmations will bring into your consciousness that you deserve abundance, and with persistent and heart-felt repetitions will imprint in your consciousness that abundance is your birthright. Much is talked about the law of attraction, which works on the universal principle: Like attracts like. In the words of Jack Canfield, co-author of the *Chicken Soup for the Soul* series, "The law of attraction states that the universe responds to whatever you are offering—by giving you more of whatever you are vibrating. It doesn't care whether it is good for you or not; it simply responds to your vibration."

The bottom line is this: the power of your thoughts and beliefs are significant. They can lift you to the greatest heights or push you down to the lowest lows. The greatest leaders and most accomplished public personas would have had their share of ups and downs in life, but to overcome them they would have had to exercise healthy habits of thinking that eventually propelled them into leading fulfilling and abundant lives, and so can you!

Weed Your Mind
Remove Self-sabotaging Beliefs

"You must weed your mind as you would weed your garden." ~Astrid Alanda

The good news is that all beliefs can be changed no matter how deeply lodged they are in your consciousness, provided you have the will, and you are consistent. Beliefs are our perspectives and interpretations of reality. Beliefs can also be handed down to us by our families, society, education, culture, and so on. We often make the mistake of holding on to them as absolute truths, but they are not so. If you change your beliefs, your reality will shift. Change those beliefs that are blocking your success. Change them because when you change a limiting, negative belief into a positive belief you are changing the dynamics of your life. This creative process is available to all of us if we are willing to embrace it. Change your beliefs, and you can shift to a new, more empowering reality. This is how you can take charge of your garden of life.

- Ninety percent of the effort is simply recognising the weeds that are present in your mind on a subconscious level. Once you become aware, you can replace them with empowering beliefs. Just as much a gardener regularly removes the weeds that spoil the beauty of a garden and saps out the foliage, flowering or fruit-bearing plants, you too need to remove the self-limiting beliefs that sabotage your success or sap out your life force.

- Examine your core beliefs. Close your eyes for a moment and try to see how old were you when you adopted them and who did you learn them from. Question if they really serve you. In case your fundamental beliefs lead you to feel that you are not worthy, not good enough, not at par, not capable – that is simply not true, and you need to consciously replace with empowering beliefs that serve you.

- Do not allow other people's beliefs to limit you. Only beliefs that tell you are worthy and deserve to enjoy a healthy, happy, and fulfilled life, with neither judgment nor persecution, are beliefs that serve you.

- Spend some time every day reading books that motivate or inspire you.

- Spend more time with people who lift your energy, and accept you as you are. Try not to engage with people who drain your energy or make you feel that you are not good enough.

- Practice affirmations to weed out your self-sabotaging beliefs.

- Set your intentions of prosperity, happiness, and success and write them down or make a visual representation, whichever works for you. Intention is like a seed that you sow; you can put it up in a place where you can see it, first thing after waking up.

When you make the changes from within i.e. you start changing the impression in your subconscious mind, and your outside world will also begin to change. So do not waste your time trying to change the outside and instead start with yourself.

Are you ready to be accountable and take responsibility for everything that shows up in your life? Change begins with you.

CHAPTER EIGHT

Rewire and Redesign

Going from the old self to the new self is a neurological, a biological, a chemical, a hormonal, and a genetic death of the old Self.

Dr. Joe Dispenza

Recent research in neuroscience and neuroplasticity reveal the phenomenal potential of the brain to rewire itself. In fact, it can literally create new neural pathways by thought training itself. There is a concept in neuroscience called 'mental rehearsal', where you have to be really present while repeatedly going over the action only in your imagination and in the process, you will create new neural pathways in the brain that previously did not exist.

The Piano Experiment

It has been observed by neuroscientists that playing musical instruments with mastery involves very sophisticated skills of both auditory and motor processing with speed.

At Harvard Medical School, neuroscientist Alvaro Pascual-Leone demonstrated how plastic changes in the cerebral cortex could occur within only five days. The cerebral cortex is the most highly developed part of the human brain and performs functions like interpreting touch, vision, and hearing, as well as speech, reasoning, learning, and control of movement. So you may well imagine the significance of such an experiment.

Alvaro Pascual-Leone instructed a group at the Harvard Medical School, who volunteered to learn and practice a five-finger piano exercise to play as fluidly as they could, for two hours daily for five days only. Pascual-Leone then had another group of volunteers and asked them to play the piece of music in their head, without actually playing the piano with their fingers. They had to hold their hands still while imagining how they would move their fingers.

Both groups subsequently undertook a transcranial magnetic-stimulation (TMS) test, to analyse the function of neurons in the cerebral cortex. The test was an amazing revelation. It was found that the region of motor cortex that controls the piano-playing fingers expanded in the brains of volunteers who not only practiced on the actual piano, but also in those who had merely visualised playing it.

This experiment pioneered the revolutionary idea that thought has the ability to alter the physical structure and function of grey matter. This also helps the lay person realise – whether it is breaking a bad habit or a belief that sabotages our happiness or success, or forming a new habit that can bring in tangible change in our lives – it is all just a thought away!

Unlocking Some Tools for Redesign

Just as a painter would need his brush and easel, canvas and paints to create his painting, and a potter would need clay and his wheel, or the sculptor his scalpel, you too can start designing a life of your choice if you have the tools and the knowledge to apply them. In this chapter, I will discuss some of these tools that will help you get where you want much faster.

Neuro Linguistic Programming (NLP)

If you want success in any desired field of life, NLP is the tool to go for. People who are in fields related to communication, behavioural psychology, and change can get magical results doing transformation work using NLP.

NLP goes with the premise that we all form our own unique internal mental map of the world around us. Every individual is born with his or her own unique mental filtering system to process the data which is absorbed through our five senses. We then assign a language to these internal images, sounds, and feelings, tastes, and smell. Our resulting behavioural response is a programming that is unique to each individual. For example, if a three-year-old toddler is familiar with the sights, sounds and ways of a pet dog living with it at home (say, a huge German Shepherd), he would grow up to perceive the animal as a friendly creature. On the other hand, if another child, who did not grow up with a pet dog at home, witnessed a dog biting a man on the street, along with the associated sight and sound of pain, it would become averse to and even scared of dogs for life. Thus we can see two distinct internal maps being created from the information received from the sensory inputs.*

So if we want to change our perception to bring about any desired change in our behaviour, we first need to change the internal. NLP works on the understanding that each individual has all the resources he or she needs to make positive changes in one's life. It

---

* Pialee Mukherjee, 'Rewire your brain', Life Positive (November 2018), p.86

is a noninvasive, medicine-free therapy which helps the client by using physiology and the subconscious mind to bring about change in one's response and therefore behaviour. A proficient NLP practitioner assists the client to achieve his personal or professional goal. These techniques can help the client discover new ways of dealing with emotional issues, lack of confidence or low self-esteem, harmful relationship patterns, coping with loss or break-ups.

Hypnosis

Hypnosis or hypnotherapy is a powerful tool which can help reprogram your subconscious mind. Some of these automatic thinking patterns that control your daily life may be necessary for survival, but there are many that have a negative impact. I see the enormous potential that hypnotherapy has for clearing away negative thought forms and replacing with positive and powerful ones. Years into the practice of meditation and a then meditation mentor, I would see the trance-like state a student would fall into when I would take them through a guided meditation, and they would come out completely refreshed. Over a short period of time, they would even make significant progress in their state of being. Guided meditation is somewhat like hypnosis.

In hypnosis, a client is moved from the beta brainwave state to a more relaxed alpha or theta state. This is called induction, and it prepares you to enter a coherent brain-wave state. In the fourth chapter, you may recall, I have discussed the benefits of alpha and theta states. Apparently, there is a lot of misinformation about hypnosis. Some people might confuse it with hypnotism, which they see used on stage by magicians or they might feel it's used for other devious purposes.

Hypnosis is a therapy, and like all therapy, it is beneficial for our mental health and well-being. It is a process of relaxing your brain waves so that you are more open to suggestions and re-programming.

Hypnotherapy helps to move you beyond the conscious analytical mind so that you can access the subconscious – a part of your mind where all your self-sabotaging beliefs and patterns reside. This therapy helps you get rid of your old issues and patterns at the very core and then install better, positive, and empowering thoughts, beliefs, and behaviour that stay with you. It's like uprooting an old tree that can damage your garden. You replace with new seeds that will take firm root and grow to serve you better. If, for example, in your childhood, you formed the belief 'money is the root of all evil', in all probabilities this belief has taken root in your subconscious. This can result in forming a rather disharmonious relationship with money, and despite all your efforts, you may never seem to make enough money. You are not aware of the fact that subconsciously you are rejecting money i.e. you may let opportunities slip by, or put a ceiling in your mind as to how much you should earn, etc. When the root cause is uncovered, hypnosis can help reprogram any dysfunctional belief. The more you use hypnosis, the more you will erase all the negative programming that you, your family, your environment and society have unwittingly instilled into your subconscious.

You can also use self-hypnosis to clear unwanted cobwebs from the subconscious. It can be effectively used for de-addiction, for de-stressing, for releasing anxiety, forming positive habits and it will also help you keep your goal at the forefront of your mind, motivating you to stay on track and achieve the results you are looking for. You should never try self-hypnosis without some guidance, so be sure to talk it over with your doctor or mental health professional before getting started.

Summarizing the Benefits

Most patterns of subconscious thinking can be reversed or improved using hypnosis. In particular, Hypnotherapy can help you overcome:

- Fears and phobias

- Addictions

- Procrastination

- Overeating

- Depression

- Stress and Anxiety

- Compulsive behaviours

Emotional Freedom Technique

Emotional Freedom Techniques (EFT) is a universal healing tool that can provide powerfully positive results for physical, emotional, and performance issues. The link between the human mind and body is common knowledge. Any kind of emotional stress adversely affects the natural healing potential of the human body. In the words of Gary Craig, a Stanford engineering graduate, a Certified Master Practitioner of Neuro Linguistic Programming and the originator of EFT, "EFT operates on the premise that no matter what part of your life needs improvement, there are unresolved emotional issues in the way."

Medical professionals are now well aware that emotional issues can affect our body chemistry leading to anything from aches and pain, rashes and allergies to addictions, lowered immunity, and even cancer. We find evidence of this when we apply the EFT process. As trauma, guilt, insecurity, anger, fear, low self-esteem, and the like get resolved, physical ailments have been noticed to subside simultaneously. Sometimes simply tapping on the meridian system without directly working on emotional contributors, the physical issue is resolved. In such cases, it could be possible that one of the contributors to the physical ailment may be purely energetic, so just by balancing the meridians the symptom can disappear. However, for the most powerful and lasting benefits with EFT, we do need to identify and target related emotional issues.

At a realistic level, almost everyone on this planet has at least a few emotional issues holding them back from pure, limitless happiness. With that in mind, EFT can be an ongoing process that we can use to clear out the old traumas and welcome any new challenges with a healthy, productive attitude.

Thousands of years ago, the Chinese discovered a complex system of energy circuits that run throughout the body. These meridians are pivotal to eastern health practices and modern day holistic treatments like acupuncture and acupressure. A wide variety of other healing techniques have also developed from it.

EFT is a simple, two-pronged process. It combines the science of acupressure alongside phrases based on psychology, where you tap on energy meridians with the fingers. The treatment, which is clinically proven to reduce stress, anxiety, fears and phobias, and past trauma, involves lightly tapping on the acupressure meridians. This not only balances any disturbances in the meridian system but also has an almost miraculous effect in activating the body's own energy and healing power.

Properly done, EFT is known to reduce the conventional therapy procedures from months or years down to only a few sessions and sometimes in less than an hour. I have found that using EFT, I can get to the root cause of why someone is stuck or not able to get a breakthrough with their finances, careers, relationships, or even weight. The subconscious beliefs or past traumas sabotage the desired outcome.

Once this core is uncovered and addressed with EFT technique, the shift in perspective is permanent.

After EFT sessions, I find that we are able to look at the same problem from a different perspective that is more comforting to us. We may even get clarity on what we need to do in order to resolve the situation. In my opinion, the process of healing is about either dissolving the problem or making peace with it.

EFT is also an effective self-help tool. The foundational process within EFT is known as the EFT tapping basic recipe, which is easy to learn and can be done anywhere. The process is based on the understanding that the more unresolved emotional issues you can clear, the more peace and emotional freedom you will have in your life.

Summarizing the Benefits

Clinical research has shown Emotional Freedom Technique (EFT) as an effective medium for long term healing rather than just a placebo effect. It has been proven to clear the following conditions:

- stress, tension, fears and phobias

- anxiety, depression, and insomnia

- help release past negativity and limiting beliefs

- effective with veterans who suffered from PTSD, reducing their symptoms by 90% in just 6 sessions. The system is now being taught to staff at several hospitals in the US.

- clears blockages in career or love

- boosts self-confidence, and self-esteem

- helps alleviate physical pain, low energy levels, and more

Meditation

I strongly advocate meditation as a daily practice. I have been practicing meditation for twenty five years now. However clichéd it may sound, meditation is food not only for the spirit but for our mind and body as well. Once you learn it from the right source, you can practice it by yourself. Meditation too is an important tool for neuroplasticity.

In a world which is spinning really fast we are constantly bombarded with an overload of information, visual stimulation, pressure to perform be it at work place or relationships, social media distractions, I think we all need a little sanctuary where we can just get away from the noise and dip into a space of stillness and calm for just a little while. You will emerge more refreshed and energised than a whole night of sleep has ever made you feel.

The main purpose of meditation is to remove your attention from the distractions and polarity of external events, the conflicting identities formed out of body consciousness and the fluctuating situations in your linear time-frame. Once you learn how to step back from these external events, you will be able to independently create your reality without your subconscious mind sabotaging your efforts. Once the mind is established in soul consciousness, it is a powerful state, and what you intend or think becomes your force.

Meditation is extremely beneficial for everybody, and many schools in the West have introduced meditation in their curriculum as it has been found to improve memory, focus, and creativity and reduce stress.

Summarizing the Benefits

- Meditation reduces stress and anxiety in general.

- Meditation keeps you away from the trap of multitasking too often.

- Meditation increases the ability to keep focus in spite of distractions.

- Meditation improves information processing and decision-making.

- Meditation improves your attention, and ability to work under stress.

- Meditation reduces reactivity and conflict with peers.

- Meditation improves overall social skills.

- Meditation brings clarity of thought.

- Meditation improves mood and sense of well-being.

However, in order to experience most of these benefits, you need to practice meditation consistently (daily). Meditation has been found to provide at least a short-term performance improvement even in first-time meditators.

Some Case Studies

A couple of cases are being discussed here to understand the scope of the therapies and how it can help unplug blockages.

The Unusual Case of Melissa Brown

Melissa (name changed) is a young European lady around twenty-five years old, who was spending a year in India. She was in the city for a while, in 2017, so I got to work on her fear. She had this phobia of "staring" as she called it. Scopophobia is defined as "a fear of seeing people or being seen, especially of strange faces." She explained, whilst it could be a stranger in a restaurant staring at her, it could also be someone she knew, who might happen to peer in through a glass door standing outside even on her own balcony. Melissa would feel a chill run down her spine, feel panic, and would freeze internally. Outwardly, Melissa was an adventurous, brave, and hardy soul, not someone who is fragile or intrepid. Since she travelled a lot by herself, this was a phobia she could well be free from.

In a 50 minutes, EFT session two childhood memories were uncovered which appeared to have an inverse relationship with the phobia that plagued Melissa. The first memory that popped up was of her around the age of five. She was playing in the garden when she chanced upon the gardeners 'doing something they were not supposed to do'. Seeing Melissa hesitant relating the incident, I decided to work with the memory of the emotions she had experienced at the time. Intense emotions of fear, sorrow, shame, guilt, etc. often lie unsuspectingly buried in the subconscious, whilst the incident causing it is forgotten. Melissa expressed surprise that this memory came up because she did not remember it at a conscious level. As she re-visited the incident Melissa recalled that as a child she had felt intense fear and pangs of guilt and shame. If she was seen by the gardeners watching them, 'they might do something terrible to her, or she would be punished at home.'

The second memory was when she was in junior school. The rule of the school was that no staff was allowed to smoke within the premises. During a break, Melissa, who had wandered outside, passed by the staff room and peering in she saw a couple of teachers sitting around smoking. One of them had seen her, so she was threatened not to open her mouth and disclose anything.

These two incidents had caused the child Melissa to form a subconscious belief that there was something horrible about peering. An association of fear, guilt, and shame had formed around 'staring.' Some EFT was done to clear this.

Later on, through a process of matrix reimprinting, the negative emotions of the inner child were released, by integrating with the present awareness. The understanding of the adult Melissa was transferred to the little child, who remembered nothing apart from the fear of punishment that froze her up at the time. Once the core is uncovered, 80%-100% of the outward symptoms usually vanish, and the person who receives the therapy can get free from it.

Housewife who Regained her Independence

Geetika (name changed) had been an air hostess before marriage. After her marriage, she gave up her work and focussed her attention on her new home, giving birth and raising her two lovely children. Her husband was dominating and was often emotionally abusive, leading to an unhappy marriage. After more than two decades of marriage, Geetika finally managed to walk out. On the wrong side of forty, it was difficult for her to even conceive of working, as she had lost much of her confidence, and she was still battling with a lot of emotional scars and societal pressures. When Geetika first came to me, her complaint was that she had a severe headache which never left her. She looked very pale and said that she had undergone all possible medical tests, but nothing showed up in the results. To her, the pain was real and constant, so the medical reports further added to her worries. She felt inactive and sluggish and did not like stepping out of the house much.

After only 3 EFT sessions, there was more than 75% improvement in her overall condition. Her headache left her but would return only once in a while. She started feeling more active. A year later, she attended one of my NLP workshops called "Create a Life you Love." The participants went through clarity exercises and NLP processes to uncover what they truly wanted for themselves, to be happier. Geetika was recorded in a video taken after the workshop, where she says: "The workshop was amazing! It gave me a new direction—in fact, I feel I now have the right direction to go forward…."

Kudos to Geetika, within a year since then, despite going through various personal challenges, at age 50 she got a job where she heads PR working with a team of 6 juniors, in an infrastructure company. This has given a big boost to her self-esteem and has helped her face her challenges in a positive way. She has taken charge of her life once more and is happy learning new things every day. The mistake most make is to expect something external to happen, which will make life perfect for them. Instead, if we step into our own power and take action with clarity and courage, we stop living by default and start living by design.

The above cases are given to indicate the possibilities that are there to uncover and eliminate blockages, and gain emotional freedom. This makes the path to our dreams smoother. However, you are encouraged to do your own research regarding these alternative modalities before you decide to go with them. The results can vary from people to people, depending on their attitude, willingness, commitment, levels of interest, and more.

Are you ready to let go of old patterns of thinking, hard-wired habits, limited beliefs and redesign a life of your choice?

CHAPTER NINE

Dream to Reality: Living in Your Garden of Life

Life is a process of creation, and you keep living it as if it were a process of re-enactment.

Neale Donald Walsch

Paradoxically, it is when you dream you really wake up. When you have a dream, a life purpose, your whole being is energised. You don't merely sleepwalk through life, but you wake up each new day ready to create the dream you are holding within you. You are ready to nourish, nurture, and prepare for its birth into material manifestation.

Knowledge without application is like a seed which does not grow into a tree. If a qualified doctor did not treat, if a law student did not practice, or a designer did not design, of what value would that knowledge be? Knowledge causes us to *think*; next we need to structure those thoughts and create a *design* flow. Finally, we begin to manifest the design into our reality by taking consistent action, and we *live* the dream.

Create Your New Reality

The design flow I have illustrated below is a cyclical process. Although you begin at point 1 and complete the circle at point 5, you can at any time choose to go back and rework on any aspect, whenever needed, and do the forward cycle again – much like the wheel – and with each rotation, you move forward.

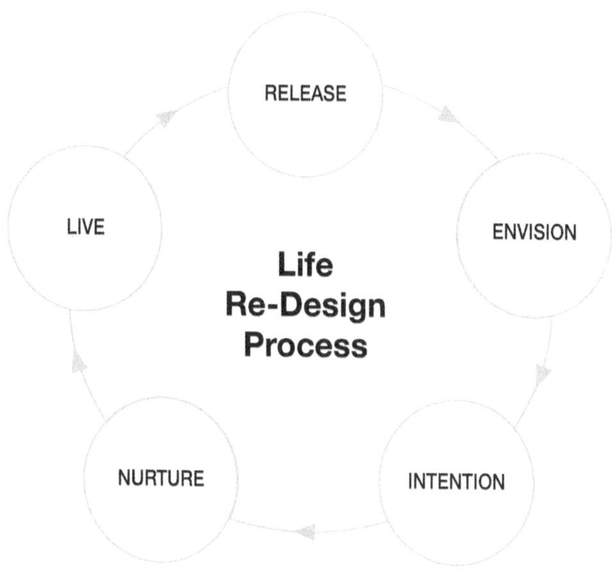

Figure 2 Life Redesign Process: Dream to Reality.

Release

As explained above, in a cyclical process, you can't really determine the point of beginning. None the less, I begin here because you need to clear away the old to plant the new. And this part of the process needs to be repeated several times initially. It is like clearing away the weeds, digging up, treating, and getting the soil ready.

In our life, we need to clear away the old emotional baggage that is much like a heavy load that we lug around. When you hold on to emotional baggage – it does not matter how much you plan, work, meditate or pray – it will block a significant part of the Universal stream of peace, happiness, and abundance that you wish to receive. Your energy becomes dense and heavy, so you will be sapped of life force energy. This makes it harder for you to move forward and make progress. You would much rather travel light.

It feels great to be completely present and free from the chains of limiting blocks, negative patterns of thinking, past traumas, or habits that keep us stuck.

A few ways that can help release:

- Do not be harsh with yourself for messing up. Everyone makes mistakes, and that shows you where you need to do inner work. Treat it like a stepping stone to success. Practice self-love (discussed in *Chapter Seven*)

- Try to be more mindful of your negative thoughts and consciously replace them with positive thoughts and behaviours. You can try reframes and positive affirmations (discussed in *Chapter Seven*)

- Try to break free of the constant chatter of the monkey mind—over analysing or nit-picking or putting your thoughts on a loop, only increase the load. Be selective not only in what you say but also of what thoughts you entertain. (discussed in detail in *Chapter Four*)

- Declutter not only physically but emotionally as well. List the things in your space that has not been used for 5 years or more. It is time to let them go. Once you do that you will observe how light you feel. Likewise, make an honest list of unwanted emotions that you have been lugging around—sense of betrayal or failure; pent up anger, sadness, hurt or grudges; constant anxiety or pessimism; inability to trust or a lack of closure.

- Reflect on the list you have made and look at it without any judgment. Put it on a movie screen, one at a time, and watch it like a spectator. Notice the experience or incident that had caused the emotion in the first place. You may like to jot down whatever pops up in your mind.

- Later on, you can take a look at what you have noted down and decide which incidents, experiences, or negative thought or emotions you are ready to let go. The previous chapter discusses a few of the processes that are available to you. You can learn the do-it-yourself processes. Alternatively, you can work with a practitioner who can help you identify and release the emotion much faster.

- You can try out a little do-it-yourself process. Identify at least one positive aspect of the negative situation you have experienced. For example, if you have been betrayed, it has taught you to be less gullible. Keep the learning and let go of the negative feelings. Say, if you have missed out on parental love and care in your growing up days, because of whatever circumstances, it has taught you to be self-reliant. Treasure the positive aspect and let go of the grudges and insecurity. Practice self-love which will help you know that you are good enough and that you are loved.

Get help where you need and set yourself free. You deserve to be happy and lead a limitless life, which fulfils and enlivens you.

Envision

Now that you have done the inner work – the digging up and throwing out of what no longer serves you – you are ready to visualise the life you would love.

Change Your Lens

As you start to envision, you have to make sure you change the old lens through which you used to see the world earlier. Instead of your fears and limitations, see your possibilities, which are aligned to your deeper yearning.

Visualise with Clarity

In order to visualise your new story, you need clarity of vision. If you wear incorrect glasses, your vision is blurred. Similarly, if you drive a car with a windscreen, which is dirty after a storm, you cannot see the road ahead of you clearly.

Where do you get started? What areas of your life do you desire to improve? Here we are talking of holistic success and not the old paradigm of success where you focussed only on your career, suppressing or ignoring the other aspects of your life.

You can do this little exercise for clarity:

- Close your eyes and inhale deep and slow, into your belly, and breathe out slowly. Pay attention to your breath. Do this 5 times

- You will notice your body is now more relaxed.

- You have your list with you; say it is career, money, soul mate, travel. One by one, bring each of them to your mind's eye. See it the way you want it to be. Visualise it for some time. Notice how you feel.

- The one that brought up the most positive feelings is the one that you should begin with. When we think only from the mind we are misled; feelings guide us better.

- When you start focussing on creating the area of your life that carries the most charge, other areas of your life are also impacted in a positive manner.

You might look for success in your career, more financial abundance, finding the right partner, making a breakthrough invention, making a difference in the world, and so on.

Change Your Story

Now re-write your story wearing your new pair of glasses. Assuming your perspective has gone through considerable change, see your life taking the shape you intend. See every detail of the story you want to create; the painting you want to draw; the garden you want to grow; the sculpture you want to sculpt.

Intention

Intention is like infusing life into your story. You direct the universal life force energy into the thought or the vision that you hold for yourself. It is important to be as specific as possible. The universe provides you with infinite number of possibilities for any goal that you choose to set. When you set a clear intention, the thought or vision does not remain a mere day dream. It begins to grow a life of its own, and together you create your new reality.

Whilst goals have a narrower focus, intentions have a broader horizon since they fuel your vision. You may set a goal of cracking the final examination in medical school with the highest rank. With that goal in mind, you can set yourself up for the competition. However, whether or not you meet the goal, your long-term intention is to become a doctor, working to uplift people from physical ailments and bringing back hope in those who have given up on life.

Intentions move you towards your vision, crossing milestones on the way. So you can set smaller goals on your path to your bigger vision. Intention is a way of thinking, and it leaves little room for a failed outcome. The right usage of mental statements will empower your intention. If you want to see results, you must pay attention to your self-talk. "I hope to become a doctor one day" is a weaker statement, than "I intend becoming a doctor."

Being specific is very important. Do you decide you want to be more creative or confident, or do you choose the way these qualities will be expressed in certain situations? Do you decide that you want a new relationship, or do you choose specific qualities in your partner and relationship you want to experience? Do you want fame and success, or do you choose what you would love doing most in life, while making your passion your career and get known for it?

Say, you love dancing and want to become a world class ballet dancer, and get to perform in *Swan Lake* or *Giselle*. Once you have a clear intention in mind, you can create short-term goals – weekly, monthly, and yearly – so that you can get there in a span of time.

How to set your intentions:

- Your intention should be practical, do-able, and aligned with your vision.

- Write down your intention, preferably in a sentence. It should ideally be sensory rich and connect with your emotions.

- Say it aloud to yourself and see how it feels. If it fills you up with good energy, then you have worded it correctly.

- Share your intention with at least one other person to begin with. This makes you accountable to work on your intention.

- Make a daily ritual: write it down in your bed-side note book, before you go to sleep. First thing, when you wake up, repeat it in your mind a few times.

- Keep a subtle reminder for yourself, where it can insidiously seep into your subconscious. For example, you can keep a quote or an image that act as a reminder on your laptop home screen.

- Now that you have set up your intention, let go of it. You should, most certainly, not be obsessive. Take your actions and trust that the rest will unfold in divine timing.

Remember, intention is like the seed, which holds within it the potential of the tree.

Nurture

If intention is the seed, then nurturing is like watering the seed. When you plant the seed in the soil, for many days, you simply keep watering the area where you have sown the seed. Since the seed is not visible, you highlight the area with a circle. Making a vision board, so that you do not forget the intention that you have planted, is like highlighting the area where you have planted the seed. Your dream is in its nascent stage and has the potential to manifest into your reality, just as much as an apple seed has the potential to manifest into a fruit-bearing apple tree. Directing your flow of thoughts towards your dream, in a positive, loving, and encouraging manner is like watering the seed. At this stage, you think of the initial steps you can take towards making your vision a reality; visualise how important that is to you and how it would make you feel when you realise the dream.

If the seed has been nurtured at this stage, it grows into a sapling and emerges above the ground. Your efforts are now visible. Yet just like the sapling, your dream is now in a vulnerable stage since it is too fragile and tender. This calls for the second stage of nurturing. You will need to ensure the sapling not only receives sunshine and water, but it must be protected as well. Along with showering your vision with an abundance of encouragement, passion and positive thought, you will need to guard against the demons of doubt, impatience, fear, shame, and other limiting beliefs. You will also need to protect it from the onslaught of other people's opinions, attitude, and judgements. However, do not shut off constructive feedback, and gather knowledge, training, and information around the subject, because these are like manure and will help the sapling to grow into a robust plant.

Live

"The seductions of power, and all the wealth, honour, and luxury it gives, seem a sufficient aim for men's efforts only so long as they are unattained. Directly a man reaches them he sees all their vanity, and they gradually lose all their power of attraction. They are like clouds which have form and beauty only from the distance; directly

one ascends into them, all their splendour vanishes."
~ Leo Tolstoy, *The Kingdom of God Is Within You.*

Once the plant is sturdy and is fully developed, it needs lesser attention and grows organically, and it is time to enjoy the fruits. Remember to share the fruits with others. However clichéd it may sound, but shared joy is indeed doubled.

At this stage, your goals and dream have manifested, and it is time to celebrate. It is time to step into the life you have created with much love and dedication. Never postpone your happiness to the achievement of your goals, because then you will feel only transient joy, fleeting away as you get ready to chase your next goal. Live and breathe through the whole process of creating with the sense of expectancy a mother has before giving birth. Although the months of nurturing the fetus can be fraught with various challenges, the joy of bringing forth a new life outweighs any difficulties.

To live your dream, you need to be alive to each moment that is offered to you. Do not fret about your next step nor have any regret for a past step where you have slipped, but be fully present to the moment, because the present is the fruit of your past action, and it bears the seed of your future tree.

Remember this process is not linear, it is cyclical. Also, life is organic not rigid—be flexible so that surprises don't throw you off balance. Change the route when it leads nowhere, open new doors instead of standing in front of the old one hoping it will somehow miraculously open. From time to time, re-evaluate your dreams and goals—they are not set in stone. Take a closer look at them and decide if any aspects might be pruned away or tweaked. Goal-setting need not be a one-time activity. Evaluate your progress, re-adjust your actions if required, bring in new elements to create balance, when feeling stuck breathe in fresh life, and most importantly fall in love with this process of creating.

Do not become vain about your accomplishments, or complacent with the luxury it has brought you, but remain humble and grounded in the awareness that the real treasures of happiness, fulfilment, and peace are all within you. Reaping the fruits is not the end of the journey; it is merely the completion of a cycle.

Are you willing to dig deep, remove the weeds and are you ready to plant the seed of your intention, one at a time, nurture them and watch your garden grow?

CHAPTER TEN

Gps Your Destination: Enjoy Your Journey Ahead

We will never know our full potential unless we push ourselves to find it.

Travis Rice

With the advancement of technology, we have benefits we did not enjoy earlier. Whenever we have to travel to a destination that we have not been to before, we just use the GPS (Global Positioning System), which gives us the route to get there and if we happen to take a wrong turn it shows us an alternate route, or alerts us to make the correction.

So before you set your wheels moving, what about setting the GPS to a destination that vows you! You need to find out who you really are before moving on to take action. Once you have allowed your true self to shine through and given that true self a name, right action will flow naturally, which will then lead to attaining your dreams. Most people rush headlong after something, which either appears lucrative or is recommended by someone else, and get caught up in a vicious cycle of frantically trying hard, hard and harder only to realise it is not something they truly wanted.

Greatest Potential Self (GPS)

Every human being, regardless of their gender, sexual orientation, race, colour, nationality or any other differences, have one commonality—it is the undeniable capacity to realise their unique potential and live meaningful, joyful and fulfilled lives. Studies have revealed that you will find your life meaningful and feel a deeper sense of well-being if you live a life that is aligned or congruent to your values. So before you set off, take a few moments to deliberate and make sure that your GPS is set at your Greatest Potential Self.

Finding Your Authentic Self

To get started, you can do this little exercise here, by first answering the questions below. Write your answers down, so that you can gain more clarity when you read them later.

- Who are the people who inspire you? What qualities in them do you admire?

- What are the qualities that you have in common with them?

- What are the qualities they have, and you don't? Would you like to imbibe those qualities in yourself, or does it go against your inherent nature?

- Identify areas in your present life that are not consistent with your values. How does that make you feel?

- If you could change just one thing (quality, place, or situation) in your life, what would you change? Why?

- What is your most prized possession? It can be a quality, or an object. Why?

- Think about those moments in your life, when you felt totally complete or alive. What were those moments? Why did you feel that way? Can you find any common thread in those situations?

Study Your Responses for Patterns

What you like, admire, and value will become clear. What you are uncomfortable with, you dislike or what you can do without, will also become clear.

For example, say your prized possessions are the trophies you won in college. The memory of one moment in your life that popped up was when you were called on stage and applauded for the success of your project. The quality you want to change is your habit of procrastination. And one of the people who inspire you is Steve Jobs. The pattern that emerges is that your need for 'significance' is high, so you will be motivated by recognition. If your present situation compels you to sacrifice your career goals, you will be unfulfilled. Perhaps your habit of procrastination is getting in the way of goal realisation.

Let us take another example: say your prized possessions are a book on chess your brother had given you in school, a bottle of cologne that your wife had given you on your birthday whilst you were dating, a very attractive muffler that your mother had knit for you, and a picture of yourself sitting on your Dad's lap holding the steering wheel of the car. One of the people who inspire you is your elder brother, whom you admire for his outgoing personality, his ready wit, his courage and loyalty. The memory of one moment in your life that popped up was when your brother stood up for you when others were blaming you for a mistake you had made in the football field. What emerges from this pattern is your need for 'love and connection.' Relationships are important to you. Yet your current job demands you travel at least 15 days a month. Whilst your biggest yearning might be to give your family the very best of everything, and for that you work to increase your income, but if you cannot spend time with the family a part of you will feel unfulfilled.

Your greatest potential self is usually what your deepest yearnings are. Whilst redesigning your life, you need to integrate your core values and set smaller goals to realign aspects which are incongruent to your values.

Align Your Vision to Your Core Values

Make a list of everything you want to show up in your life. That may be a long list!

- Now, strike out everything that is not congruent with your core value, because, in the long run, these will sap you.

- Remove things from the list which are not in your hands directly, for example 'working in a Fortune 500 company, where my boss is cooperative and generous'. Working in a Fortune 500 company can be your goal, but you can't really have control over your boss' behaviour. Having such expectations of others can set you up for failure.

- Add details which are value-congruent. For example, if your core value is growth and development, you can aim to be part of a company which gives you ample opportunity to grow in your area of expertise. If you love travelling the world, you may set the target of having a job that takes you to different parts of the world, and you have the opportunity to explore those places. If you want greater flexibility in the way you work, you might plan to become an entrepreneur.

What is the Vision of Your Best Life?

"Dream is not something you see while sleeping; it is something that doesn't let you sleep." A P J Abdul Kalam, *Wings of Fire: An Autobiography.*

Give yourself permission to dream. Don't let fear of others' opinions, past failures, societal rules, and structures, limit your vision of your best life. As long as you align your dream with your core values, desire to explore your unique talents and gifts, share your value with the world and make a living out of it, know that you are on the right track. You can do a little exercise which will give you more clarity. Write down your response to each point below:

- Visualise what your best life would look like. Write down in details.

- What are the feelings that you associate with your best life?

- Are there any particular sensations that you feel in your body?

- Also notice if any negative emotions, sensations, or thoughts are coming up, like, fear, doubt, apprehension, etc.

- What version of yourself will you need to be to live your best life? Note down the qualities you already have. In a separate column, write down the qualities that you would like to develop, like, more confidence, able speaker, more compassionate, patient listener, and so on—whatever is relevant to you.

- What are the habits you need to develop to help you go forward? For example, you want to become this very effective and famous lawyer, yet you hate reading. As a good lawyer, you need to be well informed and well read. How willing are you to develop an aspect of yourself, where you are lacking?

- What are the limiting beliefs or negative self-talk holding you back from pursuing your dream?

The response to all the above is feedback to yourself, which will help you understand what is holding you back from your best life. Is there anything more important to you? If yes, is it possible to integrate it with your vision? Do you have the courage and willingness to make the changes that are needed from you? If yes, you can go ahead to the next step.

Do Not Cloud Your Vision by Confusion or Contradictions

If you are confused about your destination, can you reach it? If there are contradictions around it, delays will happen. Likewise, if there are some confusions and contradiction regarding where you are headed in life, you will need to clear them before you set off.

Give precedence to goals that enthuse you: There are some people who have various interests and are good at many things. We often use the term: 'He's a Jack of all trades, but master of none.' Many times we even say this to describe ourselves. If our attention is drawn to many different interests and we are even quite good at them, we find easy gratification through the appreciation we receive. To become an expert in anything you need to have undiluted focus. Although debatable, the '10,000 hour rule' applies to become an expert. Consistent effort and dedication is indeed required to gain mastery in anything.

If you have a number of different interests, step back, and try to figure out which one calls out to you the most. Are you willing to spend a great deal of time honing this knowledge or skill, and never tire learning more on the topic? Once you figure it out, do not hesitate to choose that as a vocation above the rest.

Do not decide on the basis of what is more lucrative, but what excites you: Many a time the lure of money or the glamour of a promising lifestyle can side-track a person from making the right choice—a choice that is aligned to one's core value or passion.

Falling for immediate gains might have several pitfalls—it can make you lose sight of your dream, cause frustration at some point of time since it is not value-congruent, your growth will get affected, and the unnecessary diversion will waste your time, the time you could have dedicated to building your expertise.

However, say you are a designer, and a competing firm has offered you a similar or better job profile with almost double your present salary—by all means go for it! You can also consider other factors whilst making your choice. Say the firm that offered to double your salary is known to have a ruthless 'hire and fire' policy. If your dominant need is 'certainty,' you might want to choose peace of mind over insecurity. In other words, money should not be the only factor by which you make your decisions.

Do not let your little voice be drowned by others' opinions: When we are not clear about what we want in our life, we are further confused with the different advice given by others around us. If our own resolve is weak, the little voice that tells us what we want is drowned by other's opinion of what is a good goal to have and what is not. In India, it is very common for the family to decide what you should be doing, and further, the seniors in the family are influenced by the opinions and expectations of the extended family, neighbours, friends, and society.

Seek advice by all means, but it is important to get clear on your dreams and goals since it is your life, and you have to live it. Your voice is important, and if you don't feel so, you need to work on your sense of self-worth, self-love, and confidence.

When you catch yourself thinking in terms of "should/ should-not," or "must/must-not" pause for a while and go back to the origin of that thought. Is it coming from a space of fear or pressure from someone else? This thought trap makes you feel as though you have to live up to standards set by others. It can hold you back from realising your true potential because you are basing your actions on what you 'should' do rather than what feels 'right' for you to do. For example, you have been told "you should marry and have children" by a certain age, otherwise you might have to remain alone for the rest of your life. Perhaps you are not yet ready to commit yourself to marriage; maybe you are waiting to find the right man or woman; or you are not yet ready for motherhood or fatherhood and you feel it is an important role, which you rather not be pushed into. On the other hand, you might feel alarmed at the thought of 'remaining alone for the rest of your life'; or feel guilty of letting your parents down and feel bad about yourself. Which voice will you listen to?

Organise your goals by importance: Once you have gained a fair amount of clarity, and the vision of your present destination is emerging clearly, you can plan out your route—the little milestones on the way. Say, for example, you see yourself as a graceful ballet dancer, performing in *Swan Lake* around the world, having a soulful relationship with a significant other and when you both are ready settle down to enjoy a great family life, having good health and abundance.

You may observe there are multiple goals appearing in the above life purpose: career, passion, relationship, family, health, and finances. The primary focus is also clear—'A graceful ballet dancer, performing in *Swan Lake* around the world.' Once the goals are organised according to its priority, the next thing you will need to do is to breakdown your larger vision into smaller, actionable steps in its logical order.

> a. Find the right training school for ballet and the right teacher.
>
> b. Join a gym to keep up your strength and fitness.
>
> c. Lose weight (if that is required)
>
> d. Allocate time for doing daily practice.

As you start off on the journey, keep daily, weekly, and monthly goals. For example, you may plan to do 30 hours of dance lessons, 20 hours of practice, 20 hours of strength and fitness training in a month. Now break down your monthly goals into weekly and daily ones. When narrowed down, it is easier to keep track and achieve your targets, and will not result in overwhelm.

Celebrate every little milestone you cover on the way.

Add to your actionable steps as you reach different stages of your progress. Read up on your subject, find experts whom you can model (and please do not try to clone them), be flexible and open to learning more. For example, you may find it difficult to be expressive or empathise with the character you portray, so you can join a theatre class to enhance the skill.

With your secondary life goals do the same process as above. As defined in the above intention these are: soulful relationship, family, good health, and abundance. It is important to prioritise as well as be mindful of your timelines. When you act on the spur of the moment, impulsive emotions can jeopardise realisation of dreams and lead to regrets. For example, if you find your life partner, and become a mother, even before you got a chance to pursue your primary dream, you will feel buffeted by circumstances beyond your control. Living your life with sensitivity is enriching, whilst living it under the sway of emotions can be depleting. Instead, when you realise you are the creator of your reality, you will take more responsibility and accountability of your life. You will make choices which are balanced and in alignment with your values and vision.

Get Unstuck by Breaking Habitual Patterns

If you find yourself stuck anywhere in process of redesigning your life and creating a new reality just check if any of the following habitual patterns are blocking you.

- Procrastination and postponing action for another day.

- Trying too hard to please people or gain approval to feel validated.

- Being a control freak.

- Blaming yourself or others.

- Locking horns to place your own opinion above everybody else's.

- Habitually seeing the bleaker side of life.

- Being overly critical or nitpicking.

- Being a perfectionist.

- Multitasking and not pacing your work.

- Resisting change.

The Power of Vision and Visualizing Bianca Andreescu, winner of US Open 2019

This year, on September 7, 2019, a nineteen-year-old Canadian tennis player went on to win her first grand slam after defeating formidable opponent Serena Williams in a straight set. Bianca Andreescu, the winner of the US Open women's singles championship 2019, in one of the several video interviews she appeared in, revealed how she had experimented with visualisation techniques encouraged by her mother.

She had prepared herself for this win not only with her dedicated practice but also her persistent visualisation. She not only pictured herself holding the trophy, but also wrote herself a winner's cheque from the US Open, as far back as 2015.

Such real-life stories serve to inspire us and can help place our faith in the powers of the mind. This also goes to show how you too can use visualisation tools to manifest your vision. Apart from clarity of vision, sincerity of purpose, and consistent effort, it is important to have faith that your dream will manifest in divine timing.

Bon Voyage

Your GPS is set—the vision of your destination is now vivid, and beckons you. It is safe to get off the auto-pilot mode. You know now you are the driver of your life. But just as a skilful driver can drive across difficult terrains and navigate higher altitudes which can mesmerize you with its breathtaking beauty, so also in life, the more skilful you are the more amazing destinations you can reach.

Learning to Drive

There are four broad stages in learning anything new.

The first stage is when you did not even know that you did not know! Let us take for example, driving a car. A child watching his parents drive is likely to feel driving comes easily to all adults, and once he is of age he too will have the license to drive.

The second stage is when you know that you do not know. Now that the child is old enough to learn to drive, he or she realizes that it is not so simple after all, and there are a lot of things to learn so that he may become a competent driver.

The third stage is when you consciously start learning what you did not know before. So now the young adult starts to drive with a lot of attention and alertness. He would prefer not to be disturbed or distracted while driving. He will probably make many mistakes and hopefully keep learning from them. At this point driving might not seem as enjoyable as he had imagined it to be. This is the learning and practice stage, where one moves toward competency.

The fourth stage is finally reached, when you are unconscious competent. Dedication, discipline and practice have now made you competent at what you had set out to learn. The young driver can now effortlessly drive whilst listening to songs, talking to co-passengers, manouevring difficult terrains, taking more intuitive decisions when faced with a roadblock, etc. Your body has memorized the new learning and therefore it is a new habit you have formed—a new skill you have developed.

The same is with your life. The ideas and processes that you have learnt in this book may initially appear quite simple till you start putting them into practice. The second stage of learning is where you need to resist the urge of giving up. In the third stage persist, practice and repeat. At this stage you will need discipline, dedicated action and perseverance. Mistakes and roadblocks are your learning ground. You will learn to steer the course with both dexterity and flexibility, and make both informed as well as intuitive decisions.

Finally you become more competent—this is the more empowered 'You'.

Manifesting your destiny is not a linear process. You are never too late to create a successful, empowered, and fulfilled life. Like all life-processes it is cyclical. Refer to Chapter Nine, which will guide you as you move forward in your journey. When you transform it usually catalyses some sort of change in others, which may not always be comfortable for them and they might become uncooperative or their behavior towards you may change. However, try not to allow other people's fears or beliefs to hinder you or throw you off your tracks. Remain committed to yourself. Above all, despite the road bumps, diversions and re-routing, slow down once in a while, breathe, smell the roses, absorb what is beautiful in life, and learn to enjoy the journey. Remember that you are the catalyst that sets your world into motion, and the sooner you figure this out, the sooner you can start creating the life you truly want to live.

Are you now ready to get off the auto-pilot mode and self drive to your desti-nation?

Acknowledgement

Having an idea and turning it into a book is an experience that is both challenging as well as rewarding. I especially want to thank all those who helped make it happen whether directly or indirectly.

My elder son Vishwajoy, who is an independent film maker and writer, came to my rescue right at the outset when he shared with me how he arranges his storyline. Although I was writing a non-fiction, his valuable input got me into the flow.

My younger son Rutajeet for designing the beautiful book cover, and for being my go-to person for the techie stuff.

My proficient production team, who gave their best support.

My parents and my mentors who had encouraged and inspired me at different points in my journey of life. Here I would like to make a special mention of BK Sangeeta.

Last but not the least, my husband Joydeep for his unconditional support.

Resources

Allen, Paul. *Idea Man,* Portfolio, a Penguin Group imprint (2011)

Dr. Dispenza, Joe. *Breaking the Habit of Being Yourself: How to Lose Your Mind and Create a New One.* Hay House Inc.USA .(February 15, 2012)

Dr. Neff, Kristin. *Self-Compassion: The Proven Power of Being Kind to Yourself,* William Morrow Paperbacks; Reprint edition (June 23, 2015)

Eden, Donna, David Feinstein, Gary Craig. *The Healing Power of EFT and Energy Psychology: Tap into Your Body's Energy to Change Your Life for the Better,* Little Brown Book group, USA (December 2, 2010)

Feinstein, David, Donna Eden, Gary Craig. *The Promise of Energy Psychology: Revolutionary Tools for Dramatic Personal Change,* Penguin USA (November 3, 2005)

Harrison, Scott, *Thirst.* New York: Penguin Random House USA (January 1, 2018)

Maslow, A.H. *A Theory of Human Motivation*. Martino Fine Books USA (June 12,2013) Reprint of 1943 Edition

Ura, Dasho Karma .*GNH and GNH Index: A Short Guide to the Gross National Happiness Index*. Ed. Sabina Alkire, Tshoki Zangmo. Bhutan: Centre for Bhutan Studies (May, 2012)

Association for Psychological Science. "Social acceptance and rejection: The sweet and the bitter." ScienceDaily. ScienceDaily, 13 August 2011. <www.sciencedaily.com/releases/2011/08/110812213032.htm>.

Classics in the History of Psychology, An internet resource developed by Christopher D. Green, York University, Toronto, Ontario. *A Theory of Human Motivation,* A.H. Maslow (1943) Originally published in Psychological Review, 50, 370-396 (   )

https://www.forbes.com/sites/brucekasanoff/2018/04/30/can-your-thoughts-actually-change-the-world/#163a902e2c14

https://ophi.org.uk/ophi-research-in-progress-37a/

https://www.britannica.com/biography/Bill-Gates

https://en.wikipedia.org/wiki/Bill_Gates

https://choosemuse.com/blog/a-deep-dive-into-brainwaves-brainwave-frequencies-explained-2/

https://brainworksneurotherapy.com/what-are-brainwaves

https://brainworksneurotherapy.com/what-are-brainwaves

https://nrs.harvard.edu/urn-3:HUL.InstRepos:4734539

https://up-beat.org/researchers-reveal-what-negative-thoughts-can-do-to-your-health/

Index

A

Abraham-Hicks, 80

Abundance blocks, 80–82

Accountability, 27, 130

Actions, selfless, 10

Affirmations, 77–78, 82, 84

Alanda, Astrid, 83

Alderfer's theory, needs in, 48, 49

Allen, Paul, 52

Andreescu, Bianca, 131–132

Angelou, Maya, 1

Armstrong, Kirstin, 15

Autopilot mode, living in, 16

B

Beliefs, 83

    core, 62, 84

    empowering, 83

    limiting, 62–63, 71, 72

    making changes in, 83, 85

    negative, 76

    self-sabotaging, removing, 83–85

Beta waves, high-frequency, 41

Bhutan, 54–55

Blueprint for life, 29

Brain

    cerebral cortex in, 88

    energy consumption by, 36

    new neural pathways in, creation of, 88

Brainwave, 39–42, 91

    alpha waves, 40, 42

    beta waves, 41

    delta waves, 40,42

    gamma waves, 41

    as musical notes, 40

    production of, 39

    theta waves, 40,42

Byrne, Rhonda, 38

C

Canfield, Jack, 82

Change
  intentional, 19–20
  readiness for, 31
  of thoughts, 81

Chicken Soup for the Soul series (Jack Canfield), 82

Childhood conditioning, 61–62

Choices, in life, 19, 26–27
  in alignment with values and vision, 130
  conscious choices, for future creation, 27
  right, 126

Compassion, 78

Conscious change, making of, 19–20

Core values, 123
  alignment of vision with, 123–124

Craig, Gary, 94

D

Default life, 15, 16, 17, 18, 20, 21

Destination, 119–120
  confusions and contradiction, clearing of, 126–130
  habitual patterns, breaking of, 130–131
  learning skills for driving to, 132–133

Destiny, 22, 43, 60, 134

Dewall, Nathan, 20

Discontentment in life, 17

Distractions, 56, 70

Doubt, 68

Dream(s), 29–30, 53, 60, 78, 120, 124, 127, 130
    lose sight of, 127
    realisation of, positive thoughts for, 12–13
    to reality, 105–106 (*see also* Life redesign process)

E

EFT. *See* Emotional freedom techniques (EFT)

Emerson, Ralph Waldo, 10

Emotional freedom techniques (EFT), 94–97
    case studies on, 99–101, 101–102

Energy, 36, 41, 70, 84, 95, 108
    consumption by brain, 36
    excessive thoughts and, 37
    loss of productive energy, 56
    waste of mental energy, 36–37

F

Fear-based feelings, 18, 20, 42, 67–68

Feedback to oneself, 124–125

G

Gates, Bill, 51–53

Gilbert, Paul, 52

GNH. *See* Gross National Happiness (GNH)

Goal(s), 19, 31, 32, 53, 54, 63, 112, 116
    long-term, 32, 56
    organisation of, by priority, 128–130

precedence to, 126

short-term, 113

tangible, 53

Gratitude, 81–82

Greatest potential self (GPS), 120–121, 123

Gross National Happiness (GNH), 54–55

Growth, 21, 31, 51, 52, 53, 79, 127

H

Habitual patterns, breaking of, 130–131

Hanh, Thich Nhat, 20

Harrison, Scott, 10–12

Harry Potter series (J. K. Rowling), 67–68

Health

negative emotions and, 37, 38

positive thinking and, 38, 39

Herd mind, 21

Hierarchy of needs theory, 21, 22, 48–51

motivation in, 47

Human needs, basic, 48

changes in, with time, 49

need for certainty, 49, 127

need for contribution, 51, 53, 54

need for growth, 51, 52–53

need for love and connection, 50, 51–52, 123

need for significance, 50, 52, 122

need for variety, 49–50

Hypnosis, 91–93

Hypnotherapy. *See* Hypnosis

I

Inner guidance, 26

Intention, 60, 70, 74, 84, *See also* Success, hidden blocks to

to change, 19–20

clear, 112, 113

in life redesign process, 112–114

setting up, 113–114

vision and, 112

Introspection, 26

L

Lavelle, Christina, 40

Law of Attraction, 38, 82

Law of Cause and Effect, 10

'The Law of Laws,' 10

Learning, 6–7

stages in, 132–134

Life, 60, 134

charge of, 22

conscious change in, making of, 19–20

default, 15, 16, 18, 20, 21

design, 31–33

living with sensitivity, 130

pillars of, 17

redesigning of, tools for, 89–99

usual choices in, 19

Life redesign process, 107, 107–117

envision, 110–112

intention, 112–114

live, 115–117

nurture, 114–115

release, 107–110

Lipton, Bruce, 59

M

Maslow, Abraham, 21, 22, 31, 46, 48

McClelland's theory, needs in, 48

McGill, Byrant, 9

Meditation, 41–42, 97–98

Mental rehearsal, 88

Microsoft, 52

Mind-body connection, 37–38, 94

Mindfulness meditation, 56

Monkey mind, 36, 108

Motivation, 48

basic human needs and, 48–51

for contribution to humanity, 51, 53

story of Bill Gates, 51–53

theories on, 48

N

Needs, human. *See* Hierarchy of needs theory; Human needs, basic

Negative emotions, effect of, 38

Negative self-talk, 63–64, 76–77

Neuro-linguistic programming (NLP), 48, 90–91
case study on, 101–102

NLP. *See* Neuro-linguistic programming (NLP)

Nurturing, stages of, 114–115

P

Pain, feeling of, 19, 20, 21

Painful emotions, 79

Pascual-Leone, Alvaro, 88

Perfectionists, 79

Positive thinking, 38–39

Potential self, nurturing of, 7

Priority giving, 28–29

Procrastination, 31

Proctor, Bob, 41

Q

Questions to ask oneself, 29–30

R

Raichle, Marcus, 36

Reframes, 77

Rejection, consequences of, 20

Rice, Travis, 119

S

Schwarzenegger, Arnold, 12

Scopophobia, 99

Seed

    fruition and surrendering control, 9–10

    mind seed, nurturing of, 7–8

    potential of, 6–7

Self-actualisation, 21, 51, 53

Self-compassion. *See* Self-love

Self-Compassion: The Proven Power of Being Kind to Yourself (Dr. Kristin Neff), 65

Self-development, 51

Self-love, 64–65, 68, 108, 128

    cultivating, 78–80

    lack of, 66–67

Self-question, 29–30

Self-worth, 78, 128

Simon-Thomas, Emiliana, 38

Small steps, taking, 31–32, 129

Special people, 17

Steps for goal setting, 31–33

Stress

    negative attitudes and, 37–38

    positive thinking and, 38–39

Subconscious mind, 60, 73–75, 80–81, 92–93

    as hidden block to success, 60–71

Success, 45, 46. *See also* Motivation
  GNH Index, 54–55
  holistic, 47
  individual view point of, 46–47
  meaning of, to different people, 46–47
  need and motivation for, 48–51
  steps as guideline for, 55–57
  subconscious beliefs and, 60–71, 76
  tangible *vs.* intangible goals, 53–54
  transformative, 54
Success, hidden blocks to, 61
  childhood conditioning, 61–62
  lack of self love, 64–67
  limiting beliefs, 62–63
  negative self-talk, 63–64
  overcoming hidden blocks, 76–82

T

Thirst (Scott Harrison), 12
Thoreau, Henry David, 5
Thought(s), 36, 75, 81–82, 89
  and brainwaves (*see* Brainwave)
  fear-based, 42
  and feelings, 42–43
  love-based, 42
  money and, 42–43
  negative, 37, 38, 77, 108
  outcomes of, 42

piano experiment, 88–89

poisonous, 37

positive, 38–39, 108

powerful, 11

waste, 37

Tolstoy, Leo, 116

Transformative force, 11

U

Uniqueness, 28

V

Value(s), 10, 19, 120, 121, 122, 123. *See also* Core values

creation, process of, 7

of serving, 57

Vision

alignment of, with core values, 123–124

of best life, 124–125, 132

power of, case example on, 131–132

Vitale, Joe, 76

Voice, inner, importance to, 127–128

W

Walsch, Neale Donald, 35, 105

Wangchuck, King Jigme Singye, 54–55

Wings of Fire: An Autobiography (A P J Abdul Kalam), 124

Worries, 68–70

Wuttke, Marty, 40

Z

Ziglar, Zig, 8

About Author

Pialee Mukherjee is an Emotional Wellness and Transformational Life Coach, Hypnotherapist, Emotional Freedom Technique (EFT) and Neuro Linguistic Programming (NLP) practitioner and meditation mentor. Pialee blends traditional coaching methods, globally practiced emotional-healing techniques, and deep healing through hypnotherapy and energy work to help clients release mental, physical, and spiritual blocks to success and manifest joy and abundance.

Before finding her passion of enabling people transform their life, Pialee spent over a decade in the publishing industry. On behalf of the Indian National Trust for Art and Cultural Heritage (INTACH) Pialee commissioned the book *Monuments Around Santiniketan* (2009). The book was very well received and it is now held by 26 WorldCat member libraries worldwide. It is also available in Royal Ontario Museum Library,

University of Wisconsin-Madison Libraries and archived in the IIMS Kolkata library.

Pialee lives in New Delhi, India with her husband. She can be contacted on her website **www.coachwithpialee.com** or email: contact@coachwithpialee.com.

Reflections

Through the Looking Glass

Reflections

(For Chapter Six)

154

Identify some of your limiting beliefs.

____

____

____

Jot down some of your negative self-talk.

____

____

____

Are there any fears/doubts/worries that hold you back? Note them down.

____

____

____

Reflections

(For Chapter Seven)

Look at the Limiting Beliefs you have listed in the previous page. Against each one write down your Reframe. (example given in the chapter.)

____

____

____

____

Look at the negative self-talk listed by you.
Against each one write down a positive, reassuring affirmation.

____

____

____

____

Look at the list of doubts, fears and worried noted
down. Write down affirmations to build confidence.

____

____

____

____

____

Write down affirmations to break through your
abundance blocks.

____

____

____

____

____

***Note: Affirmations are given on pages 157, 158, &
159. You can create your own ones too.***

Affirmations

SELF LOVE

I AM worthy.

I love and accept myself.

I appreciate all of me.

I unconditionally love all aspects of me.

Compassion is my natural state.

I accept myself the way I am.

I am unique just as everyone else.

ABUNDANCE

Prosperity flows through me at all times.

The Universe provides for me.

I allow myself to flourish.

I appreciate everything I have.

OVERCOMING DOUBT/FEAR/WORRY

I trust and let go.

I am safe, divinely guided and protected.

Peace begins with me.

I let go fears and worries, allowing the universe to do its thing.

I surrender to divine timing.

The universe has my back.

I am at peace with my past.

OVERCOMING NEGATIVE SELF TALK

There is power within me.

I wake with new energy and optimism.

I feel wonderful and alive.

I can accomplish anything I set my heart on.

I have my unique values, so I don't compare myself to others.

CONFIDENCE

I inspire those around me.

I make my own goals and crush them.

I am a powerful creator.

I am beautiful inside out.

I am humble yet have pride in me.

I inhale confidence and exhale fear.

I can do what I set my intentions on.

I am successful in everything I do.

I find freedom in my vulnerability.

Reflections

(For Chapter Nine)

What is the dream you want to achieve that fulfills your soul purpose? (Visualise in detail. Do the clarity exercises.)

____

____

____

Write down 3 limiting beliefs/habits you want to release, that keep you stuck.

____

____

____

Write down a powerful intention. (Make a vision board – a visual representation of what you want to manifest in your life)

____

____

____

Reflections

(For Chapter Ten)

Write down your vision here.(*Be flexible enough to be intuitively guided, open to modifying and improving as your vision continues to unfold along your journey)*

List the mile stones on the way to your goal/vision.
(Also write down how you will celebrate when you reach each little milestone. Try to make each celebration different.)

9 789353 961343